Co-Workers
in the Vineyard of the Lord

A Resource for Guiding the Development of Lay Ecclesial Ministry

United States Conference of Catholic Bishops

The document *Co-Workers in the Vineyard of the Lord: A Resource for Guiding the Development of Lay Ecclesial Ministry* was developed by the Committee on the Laity of the United States Conference of Catholic Bishops (USCCB). It was approved by the full body of bishops at its November 2005 General Meeting and has been authorized for publication by the undersigned.

Msgr. William P. Fay
General Secretary, USCCB

Scripture text on p. 7 is taken from the *New American Bible*, copyright © 1991, 1986, and 1970 by the Confraternity of Christian Doctrine, Washington, DC 20017 and is used by permission of the copyright owner. All rights reserved.

Scripture texts on pp. 19-20 are taken from the *New Revised Standard Version Bible: Catholic Edition*, copyright © 1989, 1993, Division of Christian Education of the National Council of the Churches of Christ in the United States of America. Used by permission. All rights reserved.

Excerpts from the *Catechism of the Catholic Church*, second edition, copyright © 2000, Libreria Editrice Vaticana-United States Conference of Catholic Bishops, Inc., Washington, D.C. Used with permission. All rights reserved.

Excerpts from *Vatican Council II: Constitutions, Decrees, Declarations*, edited by Austin Flannery, OP, copyright © 1996, Costello Publishing Company, Inc., Northport, N.Y. are used with permission of the publisher, all rights reserved. No part of these excerpts may be reproduced, stored in a retrieval system, or transmitted in any form or by any means—electronic, mechanical, photocopying, recording, or otherwise—without express written permission of Costello Publishing Company.

Excerpts from the *Code of Canon Law: Latin-English Edition, New English Translation*. Translation of *Codex Iuris Canonici* prepared under the auspices of the Canon Law Society of America, Washington, D.C. Copyright © 1998. Used with permission.

www.usccb.org

First Printing, December 2005

ISBN 1-57455-724-6

Contents

Introduction   5

Part One: Foundations.   7

A. Describing and Responding to New Realities   7
    The Call to All Believers.   7
    The Call to the Lay Faithful   8
    The Call to Lay Ecclesial Ministry.   10
    Reality of Lay Ecclesial Ministry   13

B. Understanding the Realities in Light of
   Theology and Church Teaching   17
    The Triune God: Source of the Church's Mission   17
    Church: A Communion for Mission   19
    Ministry: Serving the Church and Its Mission   20
    The Bishop and Lay Ecclesial Ministers.   21
    The Priest and Lay Ecclesial Ministers.   23
    The Deacon and Lay Ecclesial Ministers   24
    The Lay Faithful and Lay Ecclesial Ministers.   25

Part Two: Pastoral Applications   27

A. Pathways to Lay Ecclesial Ministry   27
    The Desire for Lay Ecclesial Ministry.   27
    Discernment of a Call to Lay Ecclesial Ministry.   29
    Determination of Suitability for Lay Ecclesial Ministry   31

B. Formation for Lay Ecclesial Ministry 33
    Introduction 33
    Human Formation. 36
    Methods of Human Formation 37
    Spiritual Formation 38
    Elements of Spiritual Formation 39
    Methods of Spiritual Formation. 42
    Intellectual Formation. 42
    Pastoral Formation 47
    Integrating the Four Elements of Formation 50
    Ongoing Formation. 50
    Agents of Formation 52

C. Authorization for Lay Ecclesial Ministry. 54
    The Role of the Bishop in the Authorization of
        Lay Ecclesial Ministers. 55
    The Role of the Pastor in the Authorization Process 55
    Specific Roles Covered by the Authorization Process. 56
    The Certification of Candidates for Lay Ecclesial Ministry Positions . . 56
    The Appointment of Lay Ecclesial Ministers 57
    Blessings and Rituals in the Authorization Process 59
    Additional Considerations. 59

D. The Ministerial Workplace 61
    Context. 61
    Some Human Resource Areas in a Comprehensive
        Personnel System. 62
    Resources and Outcomes. 64

Conclusion 66

Introduction

Co-Workers in the Vineyard of the Lord is a resource for diocesan bishops and for all others who are responsible for guiding the development of lay ecclesial ministry in the United States. For several decades and in growing numbers, lay men and women have been undertaking a wide variety of roles in Church ministries. Many of these roles presume a significant degree of preparation, formation, and professional competence. They require authorization of the hierarchy in order for the person to serve publicly in the local church. They entrust to laity responsibilities for leadership in particular areas of ministry and thereby draw certain lay persons into a close mutual collaboration with the pastoral ministry of bishops, priests, and deacons.

These men and women of every race and culture who serve in parishes, schools, diocesan agencies, and Church institutions are identified by many different position titles. In *Co-Workers in the Vineyard of the Lord* we identify them in a generic way as "lay ecclesial ministers." We do so in order to reflect on what they have in common and to propose some understandings of lay ecclesial ministry situated within our social and ecclesial environment and within the framework of the Church's belief, teaching, and pastoral practice.

We offer this document as a pastoral and theological reflection on the reality of lay ecclesial ministry, as an affirmation of those who serve in this way, and as a synthesis of best thinking and practice. The following components provide the structure of the document:

- Theological foundations for lay ecclesial ministry
- Discernment and suitability for lay ecclesial ministry
- Formation of lay ecclesial ministers
- Authorization of lay ecclesial ministers
- Policies and practices in the ministerial workplace

We intend *Co-Workers in the Vineyard of the Lord* to be a common frame of reference for ensuring that the development of lay ecclesial ministry continues in ways that are faithful to the Church's theological and doctrinal tradition and that respond to contemporary pastoral needs and situations. Unlike the USCCB documents *Program of Priestly Formation* and the *National Directory for the Formation, Ministry, and Life of Permanent Deacons, Co-Workers in the Vineyard of the Lord* does not propose norms or establish particular law. It expresses at this point in history what we bishops have learned from the experience of lay ecclesial ministry in the United States. It suggests concepts, goals, strategies, resources, and ideas to consider. It invites local adaptation, application, and implementation to achieve consistency where possible and to encourage diversity where appropriate. It calls Church leaders, ordained and lay, to become more intentional and effective in ordering and integrating lay ecclesial ministers within the ministerial life and structures of our dioceses.

Co-Workers in the Vineyard of the Lord expresses our strong desire for the fruitful collaboration of ordained and lay ministers who, in distinct but complementary ways, continue in the Church the saving mission of Christ for the world, his vineyard.

Part One
Foundations

A. Describing and Responding to New Realities

"You too go into my vineyard." (Mt 20:4)

The Call to All Believers

God calls. We respond. This fundamental, essential pattern in the life of every believer appears throughout salvation history. The Father calls a chosen people, patriarchs, and prophets. Jesus calls his apostles and disciples. The Risen Lord calls everyone to labor in his vineyard, that is, in a world that must be transformed in view of the final coming of the Reign of God; and the Holy Spirit empowers all with the various gifts and ministries for the building up of the Body of Christ.

The basic call is the same for all the followers of Christ, namely "that all Christians in whatever state or walk of life are called to the fullness of christian life and to the perfection of charity, and this holiness is conducive to a more human way of living even in society here on earth."[1] This foundational belief, announced with urgency by the Second Vatican Council, continues to be expressed not only through Church teaching but also, in diverse ways, through the lives of the

---

1   Second Vatican Council, *Dogmatic Constitution on the Church* (*Lumen Gentium*) (LG), no. 40, in *Vatican Council II: Constitutions, Decrees, Declarations* (rev. trans. in inclusive language), edited by Austin Flannery (Northport, NY: Costello Publishing, 1996). All subsequent Vatican II references come from the Flannery edition.

Christian faithful. For the call to holiness is "an undeniable requirement arising from the very mystery of the Church."[2]

In this regard, the Council also taught that "the forms and tasks of life are many but there is one holiness, which is cultivated by all who are led by God's Spirit. . . . All, however, according to their own gifts and duties must steadfastly advance along the way of a living faith, which arouses hope and works through love."[3]

The Call to the Lay Faithful

Lay men and women hear and answer the universal call to holiness primarily and uniquely in the secular realm. They are found "in each and every one of the world's occupations and callings and in the ordinary circumstances of social and family life which, as it were, form the context of their existence. There they are called by God to contribute to the sanctification of the world from within, like leaven, in the spirit of the Gospel, by fulfilling their own particular duties."[4]

For lay persons, this call, given in the Sacraments of Initiation, is rightly described as having a "secular character" that is properly theirs as laity. The secular nature of their calling refers to the fact that God "has handed over the world to women and men, so that they may participate in the work of creation, free creation from the influence of sin and sanctify themselves in marriage or the celibate life, in a family, in a profession and in the various activities of society."[5] This task is itself a participation in the mission of the Church.

All of the baptized are called to work toward the transformation of the world. Most do this by working in the secular realm; some do this by working in the Church and focusing on the building of ecclesial communion, which has among its purposes the transformation of the world. Working in the Church is a path of Christian discipleship to be encouraged by the hierarchy.[6] The possibility that lay

---

2   Pope John Paul II, *The Vocation of the Lay Faithful in the Church and in the World* (*Christifideles Laici*) (CL) (Washington, DC: United States Conference of Catholic Bishops [USCCB], 1998), no. 16.

3   LG, no. 41.

4   LG, no. 31.

5   CL, no. 15.

6   See LG, nos. 30, 33, 37.

persons undertake Church ministries can be grounded in Scripture and the teachings of the Church, from St. Paul to the Second Vatican Council and in more recent documents. "Sharing in the function of Christ, priest, prophet and king, the laity have an active part of their own in the life and activity of the church. Their activity within the church communities is so necessary that without it the apostolate of the pastors will frequently be unable to obtain its full effect."[7]

Today in parishes, schools, Church institutions, and diocesan agencies, laity serve in various "ministries, offices and roles" that do not require sacramental ordination but rather "find their foundation in the Sacraments of Baptism and Confirmation, indeed, for a good many of them, in the Sacrament of Matrimony."[8] What Pope Paul VI said of the laity thirty years ago—and what the *Catechism of the Catholic Church* specifically repeats—has now become an important, welcomed reality throughout our dioceses: "The laity can also feel called, or in fact be called, to cooperate with their pastors in the service of the ecclesial community, for the sake of its growth and life. This can be done through the exercise of different kinds of ministries according to the grace and charisms which the Lord has been pleased to bestow on them."[9]

In parishes especially, but also in other Church institutions and communities, lay women and men generously and extensively "cooperate with their pastors in the service of the ecclesial community." This is a sign of the Holy Spirit's movement in the lives of our sisters and brothers. We are very grateful for all who undertake various roles in Church ministry. Many do so on a limited and voluntary basis: for example, extraordinary ministers of Holy Communion, readers, cantors and choir members, catechists, pastoral council members, visitors to the sick and needy, and those who serve in programs such as sacramental preparation, youth ministry, including ministry with people with disabilities, and charity and justice.

---

7   Second Vatican Council, *Decree on the Apostolate of the Lay People* (*Apostolicam Actuositatem*) (AA), no. 10; see also LG, no. 33, and Congregation for the Clergy et al., *Instruction on Certain Questions Regarding the Collaboration of the Non-Ordained Faithful in the Sacred Ministry of Priests* (*Ecclesiae de Mysterio*) (Washington, DC: USCCB–Libreria Editrice Vaticana, 1998), Foreword.

8   CL, no. 23.

9   Paul VI, *On Evangelization in the Modern World* (*Evangelii Nuntiandi*) (EN), no. 73, as quoted in the *Catechism of the Catholic Church* (CCC), 2nd ed. (Washington, DC: USCCB–Libreria Editrice Vaticana, 2000), no. 910. See also 1 Cor 12:11 and LG, no. 12.

This situation corresponds well with a vision and challenge expressed by Pope John Paul II as he led the Church across the threshold of a new Christian millennium:

> The unity of the Church is not uniformity, but an organic blending of legitimate diversities. It is the reality of many members joined in a single body, the one Body of Christ (cf. 1 Cor 12:12). Therefore the Church of the Third Millennium will need to encourage all the baptized and confirmed to be aware of their active responsibility in the Church's life. Together with the ordained ministry, other ministries, whether formally instituted or simply recognized, can flourish for the good of the whole community, sustaining it in all its many needs: from catechesis to liturgy, from education of the young to the widest array of charitable works.[10]

The Call to Lay Ecclesial Ministry

Within this large group is a smaller group on whom this document focuses: those men and women whose ecclesial service is characterized by

- *Authorization* of the hierarchy to serve publicly in the local church
- *Leadership* in a particular area of ministry
- *Close mutual collaboration* with the pastoral ministry of bishops, priests, and deacons
- *Preparation and formation* appropriate to the level of responsibilities that are assigned to them

Previous documents from our Conference have called such women and men "lay ecclesial ministers" and their service "lay ecclesial ministry."[11] We continue that usage here with the following understandings.

---

10   John Paul II, *At the Close of the Great Jubilee of the Year 2000* (*Novo Millennio Ineunte*) (NMI), no. 46, http://www.vatican.va/holy_father/john_paul_ii/apost_letters/documents/hf_jp-ii_apl_ 20010106_novo-millennio-ineunte_en.html.

11   See USCCB Subcommittee on Lay Ministry, *Lay Ecclesial Ministry: The State of the Questions* (Washington, DC: USCCB, 1999), 7-8; USCCB, *Called and Gifted for the Third Millennium* (Washington, DC: USCCB, 1995), 16-17; and USCCB, *Called and Gifted: The American Catholic Laity* (Washington, DC: USCCB, 1980), 3-4.

The term "lay ecclesial minister" is generic. It is meant to encompass and describe several possible roles. In parish life—to cite only one sphere of involvement—the pastoral associate, parish catechetical leader, youth ministry leader, school principal, and director of liturgy or pastoral music are examples of such roles. Participation in the exercise of the pastoral care of a parish, as described in the *Code of Canon Law*, canon 517 §2,[12] is another example of lay ecclesial ministry, although it differs in kind from the other roles because it exists simply because of the shortage of priests. It is the responsibility of the bishop, or his delegate, in accord with the norms of canon law, to identify the roles that most clearly exemplify lay ecclesial ministry. Application of the term may vary from diocese to diocese.

"Lay ecclesial minister" is not itself a specific position title. We do not use the term in order to establish a new rank or order among the laity. Rather, we use the terminology as an adjective to identify a developing and growing reality, to describe it more fully, and to seek a deeper understanding of it under the guidance of the Holy Spirit.

The term reflects certain key realities. The ministry is *lay* because it is service done by lay persons. The sacramental basis is the Sacraments of Initiation, not the Sacrament of Ordination. The ministry is *ecclesial* because it has a place within the community of the Church, whose communion and mission it serves, and because it is submitted to the discernment, authorization, and supervision of the hierarchy. Finally, it is *ministry* because it is a participation in the threefold ministry of Christ, who is priest, prophet, and king. "In this original sense the term *ministry* (*servitium*) expresses only the work by which the Church's members continue the mission and ministry of Christ within her and the whole world."[13] We apply the term "ministry" to certain works undertaken by the lay faithful by making constant reference

---

12 Canon 517 §2: "If, because of a lack of priests, the diocesan bishop has decided that participation in the exercise of the pastoral care of a parish is to be entrusted to a deacon, to another person who is not a priest, or to a community of persons, he is to appoint some priest who, provided with the powers and faculties of a pastor, is to direct the pastoral care" (Canon Law Society of America [CLSA], *Code of Canon Law, Latin-English Edition, New English Translation* [CIC] [Washington, DC: CLSA, 1999]). No common title is used throughout the United States for persons appointed under this canon. In 2004, a participation in the pastoral care of 566 parishes was entrusted to deacons, religious sisters and brothers, and other lay persons, an increase from 268 parishes in 1993 (CARA *Special Report*, Summer 2005, "Understanding the Ministry and Experience: Parish Life Coordinators in the United States," commissioned by the Emerging Models Project (www.emergingmodels.org).

13 *Ecclesiae de Mysterio*, practical provisions, articles 1, 2.

to one source, the ministry of Christ. The application of "ministry" to the laity is not something to be confused with ordained ministry nor in any way construed to compromise the specific nature of ordained ministry.[14] The lay ecclesial minister is called to service in the Church and not necessarily to a lifelong commitment as happens in Ordination. Lay ecclesial ministry is exercised in accordance with the specific lay vocation.[15]

The term "lay ecclesial ministry" does not imply that the ministries in question are distinctive to lay persons alone. What is distinctive to the laity is engagement in the world with the intent of bringing the secular order into conformity with God's plan. However, by their baptismal incorporation into the Body of Christ, lay persons are also equipped with gifts and graces to build up the Church from within, in co-operation with the hierarchy and under its direction.[16] While lay ecclesial ministers carry out responsibilities rooted in their baptismal call and gifts, serving publicly in the local church requires authorization by competent authority. Lay collaboration with ordained ministers cannot mean substitution for ordained ministry.[17]

Their functions of collaboration with the ordained require of lay ecclesial ministers a special level of professional competence and presence to the community. Their position often involves coordinating and directing others in the community. They are frequently employed on a full- or part-time basis by parishes, dioceses, or church institutions. For these reasons, their roles often require academic preparation, certification, credentialing, and a formation that integrates personal, spiritual, intellectual, and pastoral dimensions. These lay ecclesial ministers often express a sense of being called. This sense motivates what they are doing, guiding and shaping a major life choice and commitment to Church ministry. At the same time, they know that a self-discerned call by the individual is not sufficient. Their call must also become one that is discerned within the Church and authenticated by the bishop, or his delegate, who alone is able to authorize someone to serve in ecclesial ministry.

---

14   See *Ecclesiae de Mysterio*, practical provisions, articles 1, 2.

15   See CL, no. 23.

16   See CL, nos. 23-24; also see AA, no. 24, for distinctions in regard to the need for lay activity to be recognized by the hierarchy.

17   See *Ecclesiae de Mysterio*, Foreword.

Finally, when describing lay ecclesial ministry, it is necessary to offer a clarification regarding religious institutes dedicated to the works of the apostolate and other forms of consecrated life, whose members may participate in the exercise of the pastoral care of a parish or of another ecclesial service.[18] Consecrated persons participate in ecclesial ministry by their own title, according to the nature of their institute. Their exercise of ecclesial ministry is imbued with the grace of their consecration. They and the ordained work together with lay ecclesial ministers to carry out the Church's mission.

Reality of Lay Ecclesial Ministry

The reality of lay ecclesial ministry, as just described, continues to grow and develop. Today, 30,632 lay ecclesial ministers work at least twenty hours per week in paid positions in parishes. An additional 2,163 volunteers work at least twenty hours per week in parishes. The number of paid lay parish ministers has increased by 53% since 1990, while the percentage of parishes with salaried lay ecclesial ministers has increased from 54% to 66%. In 2005, the percentage of lay women is 64%; laymen, 20%; religious women, 16%. Religious educators (41.5%) and general pastoral ministers (25%) account for two thirds of all parish ministers.[19]

In 2004 and 2005, in the United States, more than 2,000 lay persons ministered in the name of the Church in hospitals and health care settings, on college and university campuses, and in prisons, seaports, and airports. The National Association of Pastoral Musicians had a membership of approximately 8,500, and the National Catholic Educational Association included 5,466 lay principals of elementary and secondary schools.[20] Undoubtedly, there are individuals in the above-mentioned groups who may be considered lay ecclesial ministers.

This document attempts to ensure that this development will occur in ways that are faithful to the Church's theological and doctrinal tradition and that respond to current pastoral needs and situations.

---

18   In 1990, religious women accounted for 41 percent of lay parish ministers; by 2005 they were 16 percent. See David DeLambo, *Lay Parish Ministers: A Study of Emerging Leadership* (New York: National Pastoral Life Center [NPLC], 2005), 45.

19   DeLambo (2005), 88.

20   Membership data given by the American Catholic Correctional Chaplains Association, Apostleship of the Sea of the United States of America, Catholic Campus Ministry Association, National Association of Catholic Airport Chaplains, and National Association of Catholic Chaplains.

We have developed *Co-Workers in the Vineyard of the Lord* as a resource first and foremost for diocesan bishops and then for the many persons who share their responsibility for ensuring that the work of lay ecclesial ministers "can flourish for the good of the whole community, sustaining it in all its many needs."[21] We think particularly of those who educate and form prospective lay ecclesial ministers in both diocesan and academic programs. We also offer this document to lay ecclesial ministers themselves to encourage and assist them, to express gratitude to them and to their families and communities, and to convey an understanding of how their service is unique and necessary for the life and growth of the Church.

In this respect we echo the words of St. Paul who drew others into the work of spreading the Gospel and relied on them in very concrete ways. The apostle repeatedly acknowledged and thanked those men and women, at times calling them "my co-workers in Christ Jesus" (see Rom 16:3-16). The resources presented here pertain to guiding, educating, forming, employing, evaluating, and sustaining those lay persons who are called to collaborate with our priests and deacons.

As we noted in *Called and Gifted* twenty-five years ago, "since the Second Vatican Council new opportunities have developed for lay men and women in the Church."[22] Lay ecclesial ministry has emerged and taken shape in our country through the working of the Holy Spirit. In response to these new opportunities and situations, lay men and women have responded generously to renewed awareness of the implications of their Baptism and to the needs of their Church communities. Similar kinds of lay ministry have developed in other countries, responding to particular pastoral needs and circumstances.[23]

In our 1995 statement *Called and Gifted for the Third Millennium*, we wrote that "the new evangelization will become a reality only if ordained and lay members of Christ's faithful understand their roles and ministries as complementary

---

21 NMI, no. 46.

22 *Called and Gifted: The American Catholic Laity,* 7.

23 For example, *Misión y ministerios de los Cristianos laicos*, published by the National Conference of the Bishops of Brazil in 2000, identifies *recognized*, *entrusted*, and *instituted* ministries that do not call for ordination. In 1977 the German Bishops' Conference published *Principles for the Regulation of Pastoral Services*, which identified three ministries by name: "pastoral assistant adviser" (who has completed theological studies on the university level), "community assistant-adviser" (who has completed studies on the university-professional school level), and "community helper" (who has appropriate general basic knowledge).

and their purposes joined to the one mission and ministry of Jesus Christ."[24] This present document serves to address further the concerns raised in the 1997 interdicasterial *Instruction on Certain Questions Regarding the Collaboration of the Non-Ordained Faithful in the Sacred Ministry of Priests* (*Ecclesiae de Mysterio*) so that the emergence of these ministries is marked by fidelity to our teaching as a Church.

The Church's experience of lay participation in Christ's ministry is still maturing. In the United States, dioceses individually and in regions have reflected together on these emerging ministries, created formation programs, and refined their approaches to the recruitment, certification, and appointment of lay ecclesial ministers. National ministerial associations have played an important role in studying the issues, sharing resources, and helping dioceses and parishes to make effective use of lay ecclesial ministers. Several of these associations have developed standards for certification that have subsequently been approved by the USCCB Commission on Certification and Accreditation. Colleges, universities, and seminaries have collaborated among themselves and with dioceses to offer degree and non-degree programs, as well as other formation opportunities for lay persons who are making a significant commitment to Church ministry. These initiatives, as well as explicit requests from ordained and lay leaders in theological schools and diocesan programs, have encouraged us to prepare this resource document as a next step in the process of ecclesial discernment and pastoral leadership.

When "lay ecclesial ministers" are referred to in these pages, the main reference point will be the parish—simply because most of the reflection on the experience has occurred on the parish level. However, we suggest that the principles and strategies contained in this document be considered for their relevance to other settings in which laity serve in leadership in ecclesial institutions.

The guidance offered here flows from and applies to the experience of Church life specifically in U.S. dioceses of the Latin Rite. In preparing this document we have consulted with all the bishops in our Conference and with bishops in other

---

24   *Called and Gifted for the Third Millennium*, 18.

countries; with theologians, canonists, educators, diocesan administrators, priests, deacons; and with many lay persons who serve in ministries at parish, diocesan, regional, and national levels. Their consultation was immensely helpful in formulating this text.

The Eastern Churches may find this material helpful for addressing their particular traditions and pastoral life.

In *Called and Gifted for the Third Millennium*, we pledged to "expand our study and dialogue concerning lay ministry in order to understand better the critical issues and find effective ways to address them."[25] In *Co-Workers in the Vineyard of the Lord* we take a major step toward fulfilling that pledge.

---

25   *Called and Gifted for the Third Millennium*, 18.

B. Understanding the Realities in Light of Theology and Church Teaching

To understand the emergence of lay ecclesial ministries requires going beyond the sociological and pastoral context. Similarly, the responsibility for addressing this reality is not simply a practical, organizational one. Our understanding, assessment, and action must be contextualized theologically and expressed in faithfulness to the Church's belief and teaching. So as we continue this reflection on lay ecclesial ministry, we want to summarize several important points of Church teaching that illuminate this reality. All ministry finds its place within the communion of the Church and serves the mission of Christ in the Spirit. Thus, *communion* and *mission* provide the foundation for understanding and carrying out lay ecclesial ministry.

The Triune God: Source of the Church's Mission

The one true God is fundamentally relational: a loving communion of persons, Father, Son, and Holy Spirit. The mystery of God is one of love, the love of Trinitarian communion revealed in mission. "At the heart of the divine act of creation is the divine desire to make room for created persons in the communion of the uncreated Persons of the Blessed Trinity through adoptive participation in Christ."[26] God then turns his love outward in the act of creation, reaching out and drawing us into divine life, calling us to lifelong conversion from selfishness and sin. In Jesus Christ, God the Father reveals his love in a personal and definitive way.

Jesus came to proclaim the Good News of the Kingdom of God, a reign of holiness, love, truth, justice, and peace, and to initiate that Kingdom in his own person by his death and Resurrection.[27] It is this Good News that the Church

---

26 International Theological Commission, *Communion and Stewardship: Human Persons Created in the Image of God* (Vatican City, 2004), no. 65, http://www.vatican.va/roman_curia/congregations/cfaith/ cti_documents/rc_con_cfaith_doc_20040723_communion-stewardship_en.html.

27 See CCC, no. 2816.

proclaims. Joining in God's work of bringing this Kingdom to realization is the mission of the whole Church, the People of God, which is itself, on earth, "the seed and beginning of that kingdom."[28]

Through Baptism we put on Christ and become members of his Body. We are initiated into the Christian community and called to a holiness of life in the world befitting disciples of Jesus. But through all three Sacraments of Initiation we are called to something more: to embrace Christ's mission of salvation.[29] Baptism initiates all into the one priesthood of Christ, giving each of the baptized, in different ways, a share in his priestly, prophetic, and kingly work.[30] And so every one of the baptized, confirmed in faith through the gifts of God's Spirit according to his or her calling, is incorporated into the fullness of Christ's mission to celebrate, proclaim, and serve the reign of God.

In Baptism and Confirmation we are initiated into Christ and we receive the Holy Spirit; in the Eucharist we share "the most precious possession which the Church can have in her journey through history."[31] The Acts of the Apostles described the Holy Spirit as a fire who bursts onto the scene and burns in the hearts of the apostles at Pentecost, a force who propels them to spread the Good News.[32] St. Paul reflects on the Spirit's presence in the many members that make up the one Body of Christ. Echoing St. Paul, the Second Vatican Council reminds us that the Spirit offers these special graces to "the faithful of every rank." By these gifts the Spirit "makes them fit and ready to undertake various tasks and offices for the renewal and building up of the church."[33]

Charisms are those gifts or graces of the Spirit that have benefit, direct or indirect, for the community. Tested and guided by the Church's pastors, with the assistance of spiritual directors, formation directors, mentors, and others, these charisms are ordered "to the building up of the Church, to the well-being of humanity, and to the needs of the world."[34] Thus, while there is a diversity of min-

---

28   LG, no. 5.

29   See LG, nos. 10, 31; AA, no. 3; Second Vatican Council, *Decree on the Church's Missionary Activity* (*Ad Gentes*) (AG), no. 36.

30   See LG, nos. 10-13, 31.

31   John Paul II, *On the Eucharist* (*Ecclesia de Eucharistia*) (EE) (Washington, DC: USCCB, 2003), no. 9.

32   See Acts 1-2; EN, no. 75.

33   LG, no. 12. See 1 Cor 12; LG, no. 7; CL, no. 21.

34   CL, no. 24.

istry in the Church, there is a unity of mission grounded in the one God, who is Father, Son, and Holy Spirit.

Church: A Communion for Mission

Pope John Paul II has described the Church as "a mystery of Trinitarian communion in missionary tension."[35] This wonderful phrase expresses the conviction of the Second Vatican Council that the Church finds its source and purpose in the life and activity of the Triune God. The Church is a communion in which members are given a share in the union with God brought about by Jesus Christ in the Holy Spirit. The reality of the Church is the communion of each Christian with the Triune God and, by means of it, the communion of all Christians with one another in Christ.[36]

The Church is the communion of those called by Christ to be his disciples. Discipleship is the fundamental vocation in which the Church's mission and ministry find full meaning. The call to discipleship is, first of all, a gift. God offers to us a share in the Trinitarian communion, the love of Father, Son, and Holy Spirit. This is the essence of holiness, a participation in and belonging to God, *the* Holy One. Holiness is nothing other than the gift of loving union with God and the sharing of this love in right relationship with others. In this way we live the Trinitarian community in our daily lives.

All believers, through Baptism, Confirmation, and Eucharist, are formed into "a chosen race, a royal priesthood, a holy nation, God's own people" (1 Pt 2:9) and so share "a common dignity of members deriving from their rebirth in Christ, a common grace as sons and daughters, a common vocation to perfection, one salvation, one hope and undivided charity."[37]

And so this gift in turn becomes a mission that must shape the whole of Christian life.[38] For, by its very nature, a life of holiness involves a dynamic openness and movement toward others. The Church exists to give glory to God and to continue Christ's work of salvation, which includes redemption from sin, by proclaiming and celebrating the Good News of God's saving presence through word

---

35   John Paul II, *I Will Give You Shepherds* (*Pastores Dabo Vobis*) (PDV) (Washington, DC: USCCB–Libreria Editrice Vaticana, 1992), no. 12.

36   See CL, no. 19.

37   LG, no. 32.

38   See NMI, no. 30.

and sacraments. In the Church we are all at one and the same time brought into communion and sent on mission. In fact, "communion and mission are profoundly connected with each other, they interpenetrate and mutually imply each other to the point that *communion represents both the source and the fruit of mission: communion gives rise to mission and mission is accomplished in communion*."[39] To separate communion in holiness from mission in the world does violence to both. For it is through communion with God that the Church serves as a sign and instrument for the sanctification of the whole world.

Ministry: Serving the Church and Its Mission

All of the faithful are called in various ways to share in the Church's mission of announcing the reign of God and transforming the world in the light of Christ. "The source of the call addressed to all members of the Mystical Body to participate actively in the mission and edification of the People of God is to be found in the mystery of the Church. The people of God participate in this call through the dynamic of an organic communion in accord with their diverse ministries and charisms."[40]

An ecclesiology of communion looks upon different gifts and functions not as adversarial but as enriching and complementary. It appreciates the Church's unity as an expression of the mutual and reciprocal gifts brought into harmony by the Holy Spirit. An ecclesiology of communion recognizes diversity in unity and acknowledges the Spirit as the source of all the gifts that serve to build up Christ's Body (1 Cor 12:4-12, 28-30). For "to each is given the manifestation of the Spirit for the common good" (1 Cor 12:7).

In its broadest sense, ministry is to be understood as service (*diakonia*) and is the means for accomplishing mission in the communion of the Church. It is a participation in and expression of Christ's ministry. Within this broad understanding of ministry, distinctions are necessary. They illuminate the nature of the Church as an organic and ordered communion.

The primary distinction lies between the ministry of the lay faithful and the ministry of the ordained, which is a special apostolic calling. Both are rooted in sacramental initiation, but the pastoral ministry of the ordained is empowered in a unique and essential way by the Sacrament of Holy Orders. Through it, the minis-

---

39   CL, no. 32.

40   *Ecclesiae de Mysterio*, Foreword.

try of the apostles is extended. As successors to the apostles, bishops "with priests and deacons as helpers" shepherd their dioceses as "teachers of doctrine, priests for sacred worship and ministers of government."[41] The work of teaching, sanctifying, and governing the faithful constitutes the essence of apostolic ministry; it forms "an indivisible unity and cannot be understood if separated one from the other."[42] This recognition of the unique role of the ordained is not a distinction based on merit or rank; rather, it is a distinction based on the sacramental character given by the Holy Spirit that configures the recipient to Christ the Head[43] and on the particular relationship of service that Holy Orders brings about between ecclesiastical ministry and the community. The ordained ministry is uniquely constitutive of the Church in a given place. All other ministries function in relation to it.

Ministry is diverse and, at the same time, profoundly relational. This is so because ministry has its source in the triune God and because it takes shape within the Church understood as a communion. Ministerial relationships are grounded first in what all members of Christ's Body have in common. Through their sacramental initiation all are established in a personal relationship with Christ and in a network of relationships within the communion of the People of God. The personal discipleship of each individual makes possible a community of disciples formed by and for the mission of Christ.

The further development and ordering of right relationships among those called to public ministries is done with a view to enabling all the disciples to realize their calling to holiness and service. By examining these relationships we can arrive at a better appreciation of the specific place of lay ecclesial ministers in an ordered, relational, ministerial community.

The Bishop and Lay Ecclesial Ministers

The bishop is the center of communion in the local church and the link of hierarchical communion with the universal Church.[44] He carries the primary responsibility of ensuring communion with the Church's apostolic tradition, of maintaining communion with all other particular churches within the universal Church,

---

41   LG, no. 20.

42   *Ecclesiae de Mysterio*, theological principles, art. 2.

43   See CCC, no. 1581.

44   See LG, nos. 21, 23.

and of fostering communion within his own particular church, the diocese.[45] In order to express fully his own office and to establish the catholicity of his Church, the bishop must exercise the power of governance proper to him in hierarchical communion with the successor of St. Peter, the Bishop of Rome, and with the College of Bishops. The bishop creates structures and venues for fostering communion with the priests, deacons, religious, those in lay ecclesial ministry, and people of the diocese. In his ministry of communion and by his ministry as "the first preacher of the Gospel,"[46] the bishop keeps priests and people aware of and grounded in a unity of one faith and one sacramental life. He challenges the local church to remember that the concerns, problems, and gifts of any one community, parish, or group are to be understood as the concerns, problems, and gifts of the whole Church.

The pastoral ministry of the bishop flows from his sacramental relationship to Christ the shepherd and head of the Church:

> The bishop, invested with the fullness of the sacrament of Orders, is "the steward of the grace of the supreme priesthood," above all in the Eucharist, which he himself offers, or ensures that it is offered, and by which the church continues to live and grow. . . . In any community of the altar, under the sacred ministry of the bishop, a manifest symbol is to be seen of that charity and "unity of the mystical body, without which there can be no salvation." In these communities . . . Christ is present through whose power and influence the one, holy, catholic and apostolic church is constituted.[47]

This unique relationship of the bishop to Christ is the source of the profound relationship between the bishop and his church:

> Every sort of differentiation between the faithful, based on the variety of their charisms, functions and ministries, is ordered to the service of the other members of the People of God. The ontological and functional differentiation that

---

45   See John Paul II, *That All May Be One* (*Ut Unum Sint*) (UUS) (Washington, DC: USCCB, 1995), no. 9.

46   John Paul II, *On the Bishop, Servant of the Gospel of Jesus Christ for the Hope of the World* (*Pastores Gregis*) (Vatican City, 2003), no. 26, http://www.vatican.va/holy_father/john_paul_ii/apost_exhortations/documents/hf_jp-ii_exh_20031016_pastores-gregis_en.html.

47   LG, no. 26.

sets the Bishop *before* the other faithful, based on his reception of the fullness of the Sacrament of Orders, is a manner of *being for* the other members of the faithful which in no way removes him from *being with* them.[48]

Lay ecclesial ministers find their relationships with the community and its pastors both by virtue of the Sacraments of Initiation and by virtue of the recognition and authorization they receive from these pastors. Their significant long-term commitment and their leadership roles in certain areas of ministry also contribute to these relationships. By reason of his ministry it is the role of the bishop, often through the pastor, to give oversight (*episcope*) to order these new ministerial relationships within his diocese and to affirm and guide the use of those gifts that lay ecclesial ministers bring—not to extinguish the Spirit, but to test everything and to retain what is good.[49]

This guiding of lay ecclesial ministries can involve a variety of agents to assist the bishop. This guidance can take a range of forms in the life and structure of a particular church: establishing standards for formation and evaluation, providing opportunities and resources for continuing education and professional development, formalizing job descriptions and establishing appropriate processes to authorize those beginning a lay ecclesial ministry, and supporting the resolution of conflict situations between lay ecclesial ministers and the ordained. In all of his choices of agents and methods of ordering, the bishop demonstrates his pastoral care for the men and women who generously give themselves to ecclesial ministry.

The Priest and Lay Ecclesial Ministers

The priest, the primary collaborator with the bishop, assists him in the work of teaching, sanctifying, and guiding the community of disciples. In union with the bishop, whom he makes present in the local community, the priest sacramentally represents Christ, the Head of the Church, and so serves to guide the Body of Christ in its mission of salvation and transformation of the world:

Inasmuch as he represents Christ the head, shepherd and spouse of the Church, the priest is placed not only *in the Church* but also *in the forefront of*

---

48   *Pastores Gregis*, no. 44.

49   See 1 Thes 5:19-21; LG, no. 12; AA, no. 3; Second Vatican Council, *Decree on the Pastoral Office of Bishops in the Church* (*Christus Dominus*) (CD), no. 17.

the Church. The ordained priesthood, along with the word of God and the sacraments which it serves, belongs to the constitutive elements of the Church. The ministry of the priest is entirely on behalf of the Church; it aims at promoting the exercise of the common priesthood of the entire people of God.[50]

This work can be done in many ways that will "shepherd the faithful and at the same time acknowledge their ministries and charisms so that all in their separate ways, but of one mind, may cooperate in the common task."[51]

Those who are ordained to the priesthood continue to live out their Baptism; moreover, they receive in the Sacrament of Orders a participation in the priesthood of Christ that is different—not simply in degree but in essence—from the participation given to all the faithful through Baptism and Confirmation. While they differ essentially, the ordained priesthood and the common priesthood of the faithful are ordered to one another and thus are intimately related.[52] Lay ecclesial ministers, especially those serving in parishes, look to their priests for leadership in developing collaboration that is mutually life-giving and respectful.

The Deacon and Lay Ecclesial Ministers[53]

Like priests, deacons continue to live out their Baptism and have received in the Sacrament of Orders a participation in the pastoral ministry that is essentially different from that given to the lay faithful.[54] As ordained ministers they necessarily depend for the exercise of their ministry on the bishop, who has the fullness of orders, and are placed in a special fraternal relationship with priests "in communion with whom they are called to serve the People of God."[55]

---

50   PDV, no. 16. See CCC, no. 1547; *Ecclesiae de Mysterio*, theological principles, arts. 1 and 3.

51   LG, no. 30. Another translation by Flannery (1998, Fourth Printing) says, "recognize the latter's contribution and charisms."

52   See LG, no. 10.

53   Congregation for Catholic Education, *Basic Norms for the Formation of Permanent Deacons* (Washington, DC: USCCB–Libreria Editrice Vaticana, 1998), no. 8.

54   See Congregation for the Clergy, *Directory for the Ministry and Life of Permanent Deacons* (Washington, DC: USCCB–Libreria Editrice Vaticana, 1998), no. 1.

55   Congregation for Catholic Education, *Basic Norms for the Formation of Permanent Deacons* (Washington, DC: USCCB–Libreria Editrice Vaticana, 1998), no. 8.

While at times deacons may carry out some of the same tasks as lay ecclesial ministers, care must be taken to avoid a merely functional understanding of the deacon's sacramental identity. Even when functions may be exercised that are the same as those exercised by lay persons or by priests, the deacon's ministry nonetheless has a distinct sacramental basis that flows from the Sacrament of Orders. This sacramental basis is marked by the deacon's permanent and public vocation to ministry and his unique participation in the apostolic ministry of the bishop.

Deacons and lay ecclesial ministers often work together as members of parish staffs under the direction of the pastor. The mutual respect and close collaboration of lay ecclesial ministers and deacons in this setting and in all pastoral endeavors can be a wonderful witness to the one communion and mission that binds all disciples together in Christ.

The Lay Faithful and Lay Ecclesial Ministers

Lay ecclesial ministers are members of the lay faithful, sharing in the common priesthood of all the baptized. As such, they are called to discipleship and "to illuminate and order all temporal things with which they are closely associated that these may always be effected and grow according to Christ."[56]

The further call of some persons to lay ecclesial ministry adds a special grace by which the Holy Spirit "makes them fit and ready to undertake various tasks and offices for the renewal and building up of the church."[57] Lay ecclesial ministry flows from an explicit faith commitment and is animated by the love of God and neighbor. It also entails an explicit relationship of mutual accountability to and collaboration with the Church hierarchy.

By virtue of their call, lay ecclesial ministers take on a new relationship to the mission of the Church and to the other ministers who work to accomplish it. Therefore, they must be persons who are known for genuine love of the whole Catholic Church, who exist in full communion of heart and mind with the pope as successor of Peter, and whose ecclesial identity is shaped by obedience to the bishop of the diocese and to the universal magisterium and is expressed by generous collaboration with ordained and other lay ecclesial ministers alike.

---

56   CCC, no. 898, citing LG, no. 31.

57   LG, no. 12.

The call to lay ecclesial ministry adds a particular focus to the Christian discipleship expected of all the baptized. Their call, however, should not foster an elitism that places lay ecclesial ministers above or outside the laity. Like Jesus they are called to serve and not to be served. They are to use their gifts and leadership roles always for the good of the Church, equipping the community for every good work and strengthening it for its mission in the world.

Ministry in the Church continues the ministry of Jesus through the ages and throughout the world. Continually, the Spirit calls forth new ministries and new ministers to serve evolving needs, as the history of the Church shows. In our time lay ecclesial ministers have emerged, men and women working in collaboration with bishops, priests, deacons, and other laity, each responding to the charisms bestowed by the Spirit. Because of their secular character, in a particular way they "are the Church in the heart of the world and bring the world into the heart of the Church"[58] as they serve the needs of the community today. Lay people working in and for the Church require support and encouragement in the special task of evangelizing an increasingly incredulous world.

---

58   *Lay Ecclesial Ministry: The State of the Questions*, 15.

Part Two
Pastoral Applications

A. Pathways to Lay Ecclesial Ministry

The Desire for Lay Ecclesial Ministry

The pathway to lay ecclesial ministry for any individual is as unique as that individual. No typical path exists, only a multitude of examples. Most of the paths are quite circuitous; few are direct.

Some young adults emerge from a range of experiences deeply committed to Christ and his mission: from the domestic churches of their families, from parish experiences in youth ministry and social service, from undergraduate or graduate education in a variety of disciplines, from participation in RCIA and campus ministry programs, and from volunteer experiences, domestic and foreign. These experiences nurture the desire to participate more fully in the ministry of the Church.

Some mid-life adults, with significant volunteer ministerial experiences in their background, may develop a desire to serve the Church in a fuller way. Retired adults, recognizing the spiritual potential of their accumulated experience and knowledge, personal financial resources, and time, find themselves free to follow desires that they had put aside to fulfill family or professional obligations.

The small faith communities of our parishes, movements, ecclesial communities, and other pastoral associations play an important role in fostering the call to lay ecclesial ministry. They cultivate great affection in their members for the mission of Christ and the Church. The habits of prayer, study, and service required of lay ministers often develop through participation in such organizations.

Involvement with such religious movements and renewal experiences was identified by 66.2 percent of parish ministers as very important in their decision to enter parish ministry.[59]

Regardless of how the desire to invest a significant part of one's life in some form of ecclesial ministry develops, that desire deserves the support of the whole Church. All in the Church, most especially priests, serve as promoters of vocations to ordained ministry.[60] Likewise, ordained and lay ecclesial ministers have special opportunities to recruit promising individuals for lay ecclesial ministry. They can invite those who feel drawn to and have the gifts for such ministry, whatever their age or formal preparation, to consider sharing their time and talents more fully with the parish community. Pope John Paul II encouraged these initiatives:

> As pastors of the people of God in America, priests . . . should be careful to discern the charisms and strengths of the faithful who might be leaders in the community, listening to them and through dialogue encouraging their participation and co-responsibility. This will lead to a better distribution of tasks, and enable priests "to dedicate themselves to what is most closely tied to the encounter with and proclamation of Jesus Christ, and thus to represent better within the community the presence of Jesus who draws his people together."[61]

Personal invitation—especially by bishops, pastors, deacons, and those in lay ecclesial ministry, but also by others who know them—often strengthens the spirit within the prospective minister and encourages the individual to consider beginning formal preparation. Assistance in locating sources of financial aid for that preparation can lower or reduce initial barriers. Invitation for all Church ministry, ordained and lay, is especially important in those communities that are still underrepresented among lay ecclesial ministers[62] and where young people do not

---

59   DeLambo (2005), 73.

60   See CIC, canon 233.

61   John Paul II, *The Church in America* (*Ecclesia in America*) (EA) (Washington, DC: USCCB, 1999), no. 39.

62   The number of lay ecclesial ministers from many ethnic groups continues to be disproportionate to the total Catholic population, although the percentage of Hispanic lay parish ministers has increased from 4.4 percent in 1997 to 8.1 percent in 2005; that of Asian/Pacific Islanders has increased from 0.6 percent to 1.7 percent; that of Blacks has increased from 1.2 percent to 1.4 percent (DeLambo [2005], 47).

see many ministers. Those who are underrepresented include persons of diverse ethnic and racial background as well as persons with disabilities. They need to be encouraged often and shown support for their desire to serve the Church.[63]

Discernment of a Call to Lay Ecclesial Ministry

Among the baptized, all of whom are called to serve the mission of the Church, some experience a further specific call to lay ecclesial ministry. The call may come in a dramatic moment. More often, it comes over time, as the person grows— within the community of faith—in love for God and a desire to do his will. One begins to consider that the graces received could now be put in service to the Church. A period of discernment begins.

Discernment of a call to lay ecclesial ministry is a process that requires prayer, dialogue, and evaluation. It is both personal and communal, involving family and friends as well as colleagues and mentors. For married lay ministers, their spouses' participation is important, since ecclesial ministry significantly affects the marital relationship. Adolescent children might also be included in the process, since they will be affected by a parental commitment to ecclesial ministry.

A variety of experiences may characterize the initial period of discernment, including increased sacramental and liturgical practices, retreats, days of prayer and recollection, and individual or group spiritual direction. Pastors, parochial vicars, deacons, lay ecclesial ministers, teachers, and advisors all play an important role in the discernment process. These connections to the Church provide a supportive environment in which one can decipher, test, and strengthen a call to lay ecclesial ministry. In effect, the discernment becomes not only personal and communal, but ecclesial as well.

Mentoring, formal or informal, can be especially helpful. An experienced Church minister introduces the prospective lay minister into the ministerial workplace. A mentor passes on more than skills. He or she presents an understanding of the particular culture in which the ministry will take place, including the challenges and the opportunities. The mentor helps the prospective minister to develop realistic expectations about ministry, including the limits of what can be accomplished. This can prevent the burnout that results when actual experience

---

63   Thirty percent of parish ministers say they were led to ministry as a response to God's call; 27.3 percent report that they were motivated primarily through a personal invitation by the pastor or other parish leader (DeLambo [2005], 72).

fails to meet expectations. By sharing their own stories of progress and accomplishments, sacrifices and frustrations, mentors prepare new ministers to make an informed commitment to ministry.

Throughout the discernment process a person needs to ask: What talents, virtues, and limits do I possess that indicate my ability to serve God's people through a commitment to lay ecclesial ministry? Lay persons with a call to lay ecclesial ministry possess certain dispositions, which are further developed during the formal preparation process. These include

- Being in full communion with the Catholic Church, able to minister joyfully and faithfully within the hierarchical communion that is the Church
- The desire to serve the Church and its mission, which proceeds from love of God and God's people
- A commitment to regular personal prayer, frequent participation in the Mass beyond the Sunday obligation and in the other sacraments, especially the Sacrament of Penance
- Zeal to live a Christian life, and willingness to live and teach as the magisterium teaches
- Emotional maturity, including the ability to sustain friendships and professional relationships and the management and appropriate expression of both anger and affection
- The intellectual gifts needed for the specific ministry
- A commitment to good communication and conflict resolution skills

The publication *National Certification Standards for Lay Ecclesial Ministers Serving as Parish Catechetical Leaders, Youth Ministry Leaders, Pastoral Associates, and Parish Life Coordinators*[64] addresses these and related qualities as they are developed through ministry formation programs. The standards are a resource that can be helpful in identifying prospective lay ecclesial ministers as well as in setting goals for the formation and certification of those who are completing programs.

---

64 The standards were developed by the National Association for Lay Ministry, National Conference for Catechetical Leadership, and the National Federation for Catholic Youth Ministry; were approved by the USCCB Commission on Certification and Accreditation in 2003; and were published jointly by the three organizations.

Determination of Suitability for Lay Ecclesial Ministry

As an individual strives to discern and deepen a call to lay ecclesial ministry, a spiritual director or mentor can help determine the individual's suitability for ministry. The individual and his or her director or mentor will carefully consider the individual's human, spiritual, intellectual, and pastoral readiness. Evidence of a disability should not preclude a person from being considered for lay ecclesial ministry.

Suitability for public, authorized ministry in the Church is demonstrated in several ways. First, the individual's dispositions for ministry are practiced within the beliefs and disciplines of the Catholic faith. (It is important, for example, that marriages be canonically regular.) Typical dispositions include the following:

- Prayer that is habitual and enriched by Scripture and the Liturgy
- Knowledge of and adherence to Church doctrine in teaching and discussion
- Respect and appreciation for Tradition and the traditions of the Church
- Regular celebration of the sacraments, especially Eucharist and Penance, and participation in the life of one's parish community
- Ability or potential to direct others in their service

Another measure of suitability is demonstrated when an individual evinces psychological and social health. Typical evidence includes the following:

- Chaste living as a single, celibate, or married person
- Friendships and collegial relationships that lead to personal and professional growth
- Mature emotional balance, respect for all within the Church (both ordained and lay), and freedom from personal agenda
- Willingness and ability to engage in disciplined study, including academic and ecclesial subjects
- Appreciation of new ideas, critical thinking ability, and ability to manage stress

Determining suitability for lay ecclesial ministry is a gradual process that involves multiple agents. Within diocesan ministry formation programs, program directors and staff are usually involved. Some colleges, universities, seminaries, and schools of theology offer well developed ministry formation programs that serve this purpose. Other such institutions sometimes rely on the diocese to supplement what they provide for their students, just as some dioceses rely on the institutions to provide academic preparation for prospective lay ecclesial ministers. We encourage such collaborative arrangements wherever they can better serve the needs of the Church, avoiding an unnecessary and costly multiplication of Church services.

References, background checks, and various screening instruments are an objective means of determining an individual's suitability for ministry. Lay ecclesial ministers working with children will be required, in accordance with diocesan policy, to submit to a background check.[65] An extensive application form can be helpful, including pertinent questions regarding personal data and necessary dispositions, space for an autobiography including description of the individual's faith journey, and references including a letter from the pastor of the parish attesting to the individual's good character and participation in the parish.

Psychological screening instruments can assess mental health and confirm the ability to function in typical human interactions as well as guide further growth.[66] Psychosocial screens usually assess relationships to authority, tolerance of ambiguity, adaptive abilities, and psychopathologies. Such instruments can be used at the beginning of preparation for ministry as well as before appointment to a specific ministry. The results of these instruments are helpful in personal interviews, evaluations, and the development of individualized formation plans. The information that results from such instruments must always be used appropriately, with careful regard for the protection of private and confidential information.

Neither discernment nor determination of suitability is a one-time process. Prayerful discernment should be the habit of a lifetime for all committed Christians. Determination of suitability will be repeated at several points throughout an individual's preparation and service as a minister. Both discernment and determination of suitability needs, however, to occur initially to some degree, before a prospective lay ecclesial minister begins any formal program of preparation.

---

65   See USCCB, *Promise to Protect, Pledge to Heal* (Washington, DC: USCCB, 2003).

66   For some employment positions, an employer's ability to conduct a psychological test may be precluded or otherwise circumscribed by the Americans with Disabilities Act and other authority. Counsel should be consulted.

B. Formation for
Lay Ecclesial Ministry

Introduction

The Church has always required proper preparation of those who exercise a ministry.[67] In the same way, CIC, canon 231, states that "lay persons who devote themselves permanently or temporarily to some special service of the Church are obliged to acquire the appropriate formation which is required to fulfill their function properly." Lay ecclesial ministers, just like the ordained, need and deserve formation of high standards, effective methods, and comprehensive goals. What follows is intended not to establish national standards or a single uniform policy, but rather to present goals and guidance, in the belief that failure to do so would result in faulty practice and problematic policies. We encourage dioceses and academic institutions to seek creative ways of providing opportunities for the preparation and formation of lay ecclesial ministers, especially in mission and rural areas, and for meeting the needs of various cultural groups.

"To set high standards," said Pope John Paul II, "means both to provide a thorough basic training and to keep it constantly updated. This is a fundamental duty, in order to ensure qualified personnel for the Church's mission."[68] These words, spoken for catechists (men and women fulfilling a broad range of pastoral duties) in mission lands, can apply as well to the lay ecclesial ministers of our country. Effective formation methods address the whole person: emotions, imagination, will, heart, and mind. It is the whole person who ministers, so the whole person is the proper subject of formation.

67　See CIC, canons 235 §1, 236, 597 §2.

68　Quoted in Congregation for the Evangelization of Peoples, *Guide for Catechists* (Washington, DC: USCCB, 1993), no. 19.

The four areas of formation—human, spiritual, intellectual, and pastoral—that provide a framework for the formation of deacons and priests provide a framework for lay ecclesial ministers as well.[69] Lay ecclesial ministers need

- *Human qualities* critical to form wholesome relationships and necessary to be apt instruments of God's love and compassion
- A *spirituality* and practice of prayer that root them in God's Trinitarian life, grounding and animating all they do in ministry
- Adequate *knowledge* in theological and pastoral studies, along with the *intellectual skill* to use it among the people and cultures of our country
- The practical *pastoral abilities* called for in their particular ministry

Level of preparation and extent of formation are important questions that have no single answer. Lay ecclesial ministers, their supervisors, and diocesan bishops above all are best able to discern local needs and to set standards and expectations accordingly, seeking always to provide what would best serve a given pastoral setting or community. What follows in this document may, at present, be feasible in some situations and less so in others.

Inadequate and faulty formation harms rather than helps the mission of the Church. Usually, a master's degree, or at least a bachelor's degree, in an appropriate field of study is preferable.[70] Degree work provides a systematic knowledge base and methodology in a given discipline. If the degree is pursued at a reliable Catholic school and if it includes theology and related disciplines, it can provide a foundation in Catholic teaching and lay the groundwork for a well-informed pastoral practice.

Partnerships among dioceses, academic institutions, and other training programs are helpful, particularly in situations where no single diocesan or academic institution is able to provide all the formation needed by most lay ecclesial ministers. The formation of lay ecclesial ministers requires assessment and evaluation

---

69 See *Pastores Dabo Vobis*, *Plan for Priestly Formation*, and *Directory for the Ministry and Life of Permanent Deacons*. In preparing this chapter we have also made extensive use of the document *National Certification Standards for Lay Ecclesial Ministers*.

70 In 2005, 48.1 percent of lay ecclesial ministers hold a master's degree or better, 51.4 percent of these in a pastoral/theological field. More than half of the lay ecclesial ministers employed by parishes have completed a ministry formation program, 64.3 percent of which were sponsored by the diocese (DeLambo [2005], 77-78).

throughout the formation process. We encourage all engaged in the ministry of formation to provide for that assessment and evaluation.

Because lay ecclesial ministers serve the Church as laity, their formation should take on "a special character precisely from the secularity proper to the lay state and from its particular type of spirituality."[71] This character entails recognizing the different life circumstances of those who are married, single, or non-ordained vowed members of a religious community. Married lay ecclesial ministers have a sacramental bond with their spouses and a commitment to building up the domestic church of the home through the unitive and procreative dimensions of covenantal married love. This bond is a great gift that they bring to the Church's mission of sharing the Good News. Single persons witness to the uniqueness of God's call in each human life and to celibacy that is faithfully accepted or freely chosen. Consecrated religious who exercise another ecclesial service maintain a fundamental bond with and responsibility to their religious communities. Amid these distinctions is a commonality shared by all lay ecclesial ministers: their particular life commitments significantly shape and form each of them as persons. As their commitments influence their commitments in ministry, so they affect their formation for ministry.

Formators (those responsible for the human, spiritual, intellectual, and pastoral formation) will want to recognize and tap the life experiences of lay ecclesial ministers: for example, their broad and varied family relationships, the ordinary responsibilities of daily chores, or the financial challenges of educating children or providing for retirement.

Every person preparing for lay ecclesial ministry has already been formed by the cultural context(s) which that person has experienced. Formation programs need to be mindful of the words of Pope John Paul II: that formation should "take the greatest account of local human culture, which contributes to formation itself. . . . Attention should be paid to diverse cultures which can exist in one and the same people or nation at the same time."[72] Formators can help participants discern the lights in the culture and how to strengthen them in ministry. Participants should also study the shadows in the culture, particularly those that make up the "culture of death," exploring how to transform them in accord with the message of the Gospel and the teachings of the Church.

---

71   AA, no. 29.

72   CL, no. 63.

Formation programs will do well to incorporate, consciously and intentionally, persons of different cultures and to prepare people for service in different cultural communities. A multicultural emphasis should pervade the content, methods, goals, and design of formation programs. Programs that operate from a single cultural model miss a dimension of the richness available only through a living experience of many cultures. The increasing cultural diversity of the Church in our country calls for a similar diversity in the preparation of its lay ecclesial ministers. Within the diversity, however, we are called not to seek to assimilate all into a single culture, but rather to join together in building up the culture of the Church—the transforming power of the Gospel.

Human Formation

GOAL: *Human formation seeks to develop the lay ecclesial minister's human qualities and character, fostering a healthy and well-balanced personality, for the sake of both personal growth and ministerial service.*

Elements of Human Formation

Human formation, meant to lead lay ecclesial ministers toward greater maturity as adults and as ministers of the Church, includes the following:

- A *basic understanding of self and others* that can help lay ecclesial ministers relate more authentically with God and others
- *Psychological health*, marked by integrity, appropriate interpersonal boundaries, and the ability to honor and safeguard the trust that people place in them as Church ministers
- A *mature sexuality*, which cultivates the expression of chastity appropriate to their state of life, understands and respects appropriate sexual boundaries, and recognizes the grave psychological and legal consequences of inappropriate sexual behavior, including harassment and abuse
- *Physical health,* including an overall balance in one's life and ministry marked by practices of wellness
- *Knowledge of one's personal gifts and special charisms* and their relationship to particular ministries

- *Recognition of the traits and abilities one lacks*, leading to the goal of collaborating well with those who have different, complementary gifts
- *Understanding of family systems and dynamics* within the context of the Church's teaching on the role and mission of the Christian family
- *Ability to learn from both praise and criticism*, receiving and assessing both with honesty and equanimity
- *Appreciation and valuing of racial, ethnic, and cultural diversity*
- *A genuine respect and concern for others*, rooted in the example of Jesus and the Church's teaching of the Gospel of Life and on the dignity of the human person
- *Virtues of Christian discipleship*, including the cardinal virtues of prudence, justice, fortitude, and temperance, as well as honesty, humility, compassion, initiative, courage, vision, energy, hospitality, and Christian joy—all necessary to direct others

Methods of Human Formation

Human formation happens first and foremost through human contact with persons whose example or advice can show one what it means to be Christlike. To the extent that program formators can fulfill this role, they will aid the work of human formation.

- *Participation in a small faith community.* Small faith communities provide opportunities for support and accountability. Creating, guiding, and supporting small communities within formation programs furthers the work of human formation.
- *Affirmation and critique.* Informal conversation, comments in class and on papers, academic advising, mentoring sessions, and peer review can further discernment and growth on all sides.
- *Periodic feedback.* Peer feedback, simple personality profiles or more extensive psychological testing, summative evaluations, and recommendations can help students to discern their own readiness for ministry.
- *Counseling.* Counseling can be a means of personal growth and problem solving. However, if psychotherapy is called for, it is normally better to complete this before presenting oneself or continuing in ministry preparation.
- *Fostering of self-reflection and self-awareness.* These abilities can be developed in a ministry setting through journaling, pastoral supervision, and other means.

Spiritual Formation

GOAL: *Spiritual formation aims to arouse and animate true hunger for holiness, desire for union with the Father through Christ in the Spirit, daily growing in love of God and neighbor in life and ministry, and the practices of prayer and spirituality that foster these attitudes and dispositions. It promotes and strengthens that fundamental conversion that places God, and not oneself, at the center of one's life. Openness to this ongoing conversion is a prerequisite for fruitful spiritual formation.*

A personal experience in and through the Church of the love of the Father in Christ and through his Spirit is foundational for all ministry, as it is for true discipleship. If ministry does not flow from a personal encounter and ongoing relationship with the Lord, then no matter how "accomplished" it may be in its methods and activities, that ministry will lack the vital soul and source needed to bear lasting fruit.

Nothing can substitute for this true conversion and personal encounter with Christ. Spiritual formation cannot produce it, for it is God's gracious gift; but spiritual formation can teach and help those who seek it, prepare them to receive it, and, when it is given, develop its fruits in their lives and ministry. This dynamic of spiritual growth is an essential component of formation for ministry.

Lay ecclesial ministry has no single spirituality, beyond common grounding in God's word and the sacraments, in the pastoral life and communion of the Church, and in the one Spirit who has been given to all. For "there are as many paths of prayer as there are persons who pray," even as "it is the same Spirit acting in all and with all."[73] The multiple demands of family and community responsibilities may occasionally challenge some lay ecclesial ministers in their effort to set aside regular time and space for spiritual practices. However, when daily life is lived intentionally and reflectively in light of the Gospel of Jesus Christ, it is a school of holiness.

---

73   CCC, no. 2672.

Elements of Spiritual Formation

- *A living union with Christ.* For all the baptized, this union is the goal of their Christian life. For lay ecclesial ministers, it is the ground of their ministry and the irreplaceable source of its authenticity and fruitfulness.

- *Spiritual formation built on the word of God.* Reading, studying, and meditating on and praying with Scripture are core practices for Christian discipleship and are essential for lay ecclesial ministers. Deep attention to the word proclaimed at Liturgy, *lectio divina*, praying of the psalms, and participation in faith-sharing groups can strengthen one's identity and spirituality as an ecclesial minister.

- *Spiritual formation based on the Liturgy, especially the sacraments.* Celebration and study of the liturgical year will unfold "the whole mystery of Christ"[74] and deepen one's appreciation of God's ongoing presence in ordinary time and liturgical seasons. With a spirituality rooted in the Sacraments of Initiation, the minister encounters Christ and his grace in the Eucharist, expresses and grows in faith, strengthens the bond with the Church, and receives nourishment to fulfill the mission. In the Sacrament of Penance, which the minister receives often, he or she finds "a personal encounter with the crucified, forgiving Christ," and honors Christ's "right to meet each one of us in that key moment in the soul's life constituted by the moment of conversion and forgiveness."[75] Praying the Liturgy of the Hours is another means to unite the lay ecclesial minister with the universal Church.

- *An incarnational spirituality of presence, and a paschal spirituality of loving service.* Incarnational love willingly enters into the "joys and hopes, the grief and anguish"[76] of the people of our time, making one as fully and faithfully present to every person and culture as Christ is. Paschal love, which always includes the cross, means that one is ready to sacrifice self so that others may experience

---

74 Second Vatican Council, *Constitution on the Sacred Liturgy* (*Sacrosanctum Concilium*) (SC), no. 102.

75 John Paul II, *Redeemer of Man* (*Redemptor Hominis*) (Washington, DC: USCCB–Libreria Editrice Vaticana, 1979), no. 20.

76 GS, no. 1.

God's abundant life, and so that all together, strengthened by hope, may hasten to the Resurrection.[77]

- *An awareness of sin.* In times characterized by a weakening or loss of the sense of sin, sound spirituality must cultivate the "restoration of a proper sense of sin"[78] so that one can hear the Gospel of mercy with grateful joy, genuine repentance, and renewed conversion.

- A *spirituality for suffering.* To minister with those who suffer or whose loved ones suffer, indeed in the face of their own suffering, lay ecclesial ministers need an informed theological view of suffering and a mature spirituality strengthened by faith and hope to be able to face and embrace this mystery of human existence.

- A *Marian spirituality.* Mary perfectly models "a spiritual and apostolic life," dealing with family concerns and tasks, remaining intimately united to her Son, cooperating in his saving work.[79] "The theological significance of Mary appears in the Church. . . . Mary is the Church in person, and the Church as a whole embodies what Mary, as a person, anticipates."[80] Devotion to Mary will help the lay ecclesial minister better understand and love the Church.

- *Love for the Church.* We learn to love the Church by looking at her with the eyes of Jesus, "who loved the Church and gave himself up for her" (Eph 5:25). Though it is made up of all of us sinful human beings, Christ has made the Church his Mystical Body. Living by the victory of his Resurrection, the Church is a reality of faith, manifested in the witness of so many martyrs and saints, in the good lives of countless Christians, in the holiness of the teaching and the gifts given by Christ. Those called to lay ecclesial ministry can respond if they are aware that the Church is God's love at work in the world, God's offer of salvation uniquely through Christ. This requires in the lay ecclesial minister a sense of gratitude for the Church, which is the gift of God who upholds and renews her.

---

77 See GS, no. 22.

78 John Paul II, *On Reconciliation and Penance in the Mission of the Church Today* (*Reconciliatio et Paenitentia*) (Vatican City, 1984), no. 18, http://www.vatican.va/holy_father/john_paul_ii/apost_exhortations/documents/hf_jp-ii_exh_02121984_reconciliatio-et-paenitentia_en.html.

79 AA, no. 4.

80 Cardinal Joseph Ratzinger (now Benedict XVI), *God and the World: A Conversation with Peter Seewald* (San Francisco, CA: Ignatius Press, 2002), 353.

Love for the Church means rejoicing in what Christ has made the Church and allowing that to shape one's identity. It does not mean that one needs to deny the dark sides of the Church's history nor think that in every circumstance the words and actions of her representatives, including lay ecclesial ministers, have to be greeted with admiration.

Lay ecclesial ministers serve publicly in the local church, so they need to accept this role with fidelity and loyalty and be able to fill it with integrity, fully versed in authentic Church teaching, supportive of it, able to defend it, and present it with clarity. Spiritual formation can help persons discern if this calling is for them, embrace it with joy if it is, or move on in peace if it is not.

- *Devotion to the Eucharist.* In his 2003 book *God Is Near Us*, Pope Benedict XVI (then-Cardinal Joseph Ratzinger) stresses that the Eucharist in its communitarian and personal dimensions is the heart of the Church. Especially inviting Catholics to rediscover Eucharistic adoration, he uses the words of his predecessor, Pope John Paul II, which were originally addressed to priests but which apply strikingly to lay ecclesial ministers:

> Let all pastoral activity be nourished by [Eucharistic adoration], and may it also be food for ourselves and for all the priests who collaborate with us, and, likewise, for the whole of the communities entrusted to us. In this practice there should thus be revealed, almost at every step, that close relationship between the Church's spiritual and apostolic vitality and the Eucharist, understood in its profound significance.[81]

- *An ecumenical spirit.* A good understanding of the meaning of the Sacrament of Baptism is important for appreciation of the real but partial communion that other Christians and their Churches and communities have with the Catholic Church. This understanding is helped where the Church authorities have recognized the Baptism of other Churches and communities. On the basis of Baptism it may be possible to give, with other Christians, a certain common witness. Prayer with fellow Christians and for the unity of the Church enriches all who participate. Works of service and the promotion of justice are often strengthened when undertaken by members of many Christian Churches.

---

81 John Paul II, *The Eucharistic Mystery in the Life of the Church and of the Priest* (*Dominicae Cenae*) (1980), quoted in Cardinal Joseph Ratzinger (now Benedict XVI), *God Is Near Us* (San Francisco, CA: Ignatius Press, 2003), 99.

Methods of Spiritual Formation

- *Daily prayer and spiritual practices.* Formation programs provide opportunities for lay ecclesial ministers to experience a wide range of prayer forms, including vocal, meditative, and contemplative prayer; use of icons or other religious images; and practices of family prayer and domestic spirituality. They should also give expression to the rich range of ethnic or cultural prayer practices and popular devotions present among program participants or in their dioceses or regions of the country. Retreats and days of reflection are an essential component in all ministry formation programs. Goal setting and assessment may be part of these experiences.

- *Spiritual direction.* Formation and regular spiritual direction is necessary for those who serve in the Church. Lay ecclesial ministers must grow in awareness of the movement of grace in their lives and the call to holiness. Formation programs should assist participants in making use of this valuable, if not essential, spiritual discipline, helping them to identify qualified spiritual directors.

- *Faith sharing and theological reflection.* Sharing faith among program participants provides mutual support and encouragement and builds bonds of community. Theological reflection, which is more systematic and comprehensive, attends to experience in the light of faith, culture, and the teaching of the Church and helps participants to recognize the movement of God in their lives and ministry.

- *The practice of justice and charity.* When formation program participants perform corporal or spiritual works of mercy and take action on behalf of justice, they fulfill the Lord's command and deepen their spiritual growth. Prayer and reflection before and after such activities further enhances growth.

- *Studying the lives of the saints.* Celebrating the sanctoral cycle of the liturgical year, learning about the saints, and praying to them will reveal the shape and pattern of a well-formed Christian character.

Intellectual Formation

GOAL: *Intellectual formation seeks to develop the lay ecclesial minister's understanding and appreciation of the Catholic faith, which is rooted in God's revelation and embodied in the living tradition of the Church. It consists chiefly of study of the sacred sciences but draws also upon a wide range of other disciplines: philosophy, literature and the arts, psychology, sociology, counseling, medical ethics, culture and language studies, business administration, leadership and organizational development, law, and so on. While the sacred sciences are the main focus here, we recognize the value of these other disciplines and encourage their study and use whenever relevant for effective ministry.*[82]

Preliminary Considerations

Theology for Ministry

Formation for lay ecclesial ministry is a journey beyond catechesis into theological study. An important task for ministry formation is to provide a more complete and systematic study of the essentials of the faith. Individuals preparing for ministry should have a sound knowledge of the *Catechism of the Catholic Church* and the *United States Catholic Catechism for Adults*.[83] Some laity may not have sufficient catechetical formation to undertake theological study. For them, formation for lay ecclesial ministry will also serve as a truly deep and thorough catechesis, providing a more complete and systematic study of the essentials of faith. This important task is to be fulfilled by ministry formation programs.

However, lay ecclesial ministers need more than thorough adult faith formation; they need proper theological study that builds on and goes beyond the work of catechesis. Those who embark on formation, whether in academic degree or diocesan certificate programs, should understand this need, recognize its benefits, and be open to the demands such study will place upon them.

Theological study of the faith employs principles and methods proper to the various branches of theological scholarship and research. It goes beyond the basics to explore current developments and the issues they raise. It questions and probes the faith and its theological expressions. It also unearths treasures in the Tradition and sheds light on the Church's teaching by making connections within and beyond the discipline of theology.

Theology delves into the Church's faith in a scholarly way, interpreting it according to the witness of the Scriptures and Tradition and making it understandable to the times. Authentic Catholic theology is always done within the Church. Persons new to systematic theological study of this kind may find it challenging.

---

82   Some of these disciplines are treated in more detail in the section on "Pastoral Formation" elsewhere in this document.

83   USCCB, *United States Catholic Catechism for Adults* (Washington, DC: USCCB, in press). The *United States Catholic Catechism for Adults* was granted a *recognitio* in November 2005.

Formators should help them to appreciate the validity, scope, limits, and value of such study and to learn how to grow from it as a form of response to God's call to Christian maturity.[84]

Lay ecclesial ministers engage in theological study for the sake of a broadened and deepened faith and a better-grounded and informed ministry. As much as possible, the range, depth, discipline, and vigor of Catholic theology, past and present, as understood in historical and cultural context, should be made accessible to those in formation, consistent with their capacity and ways of learning. Thus, their faith, spirituality, and pastoral practice can be strengthened, and they will become theologically well-formed pastoral ministers: knowing the breadth of Church teaching and the richly varied theological tradition, and able to access and use these resources to meet the needs of ministry today.

An Ecumenical and Interfaith Dimension

The ecumenical and interfaith dimensions of intellectual formation are particularly important as our society becomes more pluralistic and more secularized. For Catholics, dialogue, both ecumenical and interreligious, is an inherent dimension of evangelization. This does not mean, of course, that dialogue is a means of proselytism. With fellow Christians it is a means of both preparing for common witness to Christ in the world and of removing obstacles to the full, visible unity of the Church for which Christ prayed.[85]

Lay ecclesial ministers, under the leadership of the bishop of their diocese, have a role in implementing the commitment of the Catholic Church to the restoration of unity among all Christians. Therefore, they should be well acquainted with the Catholic principles on ecumenism as set forth in the Second Vatican Council's Decree on Ecumenism (Unitatis Redintegratio), the Pontifical Council for Promoting Christian Unity's Directory for the Application of Principles and Norms on Ecumenism,[86] and Pope John Paul II's encyclical That They May Be One (Ut Unum Sint). They will also be helped by the recommendations and guidelines given in

---

84   See Called and Gifted for the Third Millennium, 21.

85   See USCCB, Catholic Evangelization in an Ecumenical and Interreligious Society (Washington, DC: USCCB, 2004); John Paul II, "Linking Evangelization and Ecumenism" (June 22, 1996), Origins 26, no. 9 (August 1, 1996): 139-141.

86   Pontifical Council for Promoting Christian Unity, Directory for the Application of Principles and Norms on Ecumenism (Washington, DC: USCCB–Libreria Editrice Vaticana, 1993).

the study document *Ecumenical Formation of Pastoral Workers*,[87] prepared by the Pontifical Council for Christian Unity. That study document identified three key elements of this ecumenical dimension:

- *Hermeneutics*. This element entails learning "how to distinguish between the 'deposit of faith' and the ways these truths are formulated" so that one can "determine whether different theological formulations are complementary rather than contradictory."[88]
- *The hierarchy of truths*.[89] This concept, articulated at the Second Vatican Council and subsequently further developed, helps Catholics to understand the faith in its proper structure and relations, present the faith to others in right proportion and balance, and intelligently compare Catholic and non-Catholic doctrines.
- *The fruits of ecumenical dialogues*. Agreed statements that have been formulated since the Second Vatican Council and accepted by the respective churches have set forth the common ground we share with other churches and ecclesial communities, continuing points of disagreement, and progress toward improved mutual understanding.

In addition to an understanding of the traditions of our Christian brothers and sisters, lay ecclesial ministers also need an understanding and appreciation of the other religions present throughout the world and increasingly in our own society, including but not limited to Judaism and Islam. Catholic formation makes a clear distinction between ecumenical dialogue which has as its goal full ecclesial communion and the important interreligious dialogue which has as its goal mutual respect, collaboration, and peace.

Elements of Intellectual Formation

Intellectual formation should be as broad and deep as possible, with exposure to the vast range of topics and subjects that constitute Catholic theology.

---

87 See Pontifical Council for Christian Unity, *Ecumenical Formation of Pastoral Workers* (Washington, DC: USCCB, 1998).

88 *Ecumenical Formation of Pastoral Workers*, 8. See also UUS, no. 38.

89 See Second Vatican Council, *Decree on Ecumenism* (*Unitatis Redintegratio*) (UR), no. 11.

It should be balanced and integrated with a "discernible and coherent unity."[90] The USCCB Commission on Certification and Accreditation has provided guidance for ministry formation programs in this regard.[91] The following are core elements to be included, to varying extents, within all programs.

- *Scripture and its interpretation.* This element includes the historical and social contexts of the biblical writings, recognition of their literary forms, and the Catholic exegetical tradition of the Fathers of the Church and the medieval commentaries.
- *Dogmatic theology.* This includes the Trinity, Christology, ecclesiology, Christian anthropology, and eschatology.
- *Church history.*
- *Liturgical and sacramental theology.*
- *Moral theology and Catholic social teaching.*
- *Pastoral theology.* This dimension seeks guiding principles for the practice of ministry in a given context.
- *Spirituality.* Spiritual intellectual formation includes the history of Christian religious experience and diverse types of spirituality.
- *Canon law.* Canon law study should in particular cover those elements relevant to the lives of the faithful, such as their canonical rights and responsibilities, the sacramental life of the Church, and diocesan and parish structures.

Methods for Intellectual Formation

Adult learners need a variety of learning methods that maximize participation and draw on participants' experience. These may include small groups, lectures, discussions, independent research, guided learning projects, theological reflection on field experience, and use of technology (e.g., teleconferencing, distance learning).

---

90   *Program for Priestly Formation*, 5th ed. At this writing, the fifth edition of the *Program for Priestly Formation* had been approved by the United States Conference of Catholic Bishops and was in the process of finalizing the *recognitio* from the Holy See.

91   See USCCB Commission on Certification and Accreditation (CCA), *Accreditation Handbook for Ministry Formation Programs* (St. Francis, WI: USCCB-CCA, 2003), 2-2.

Pastoral Formation

GOAL: *Pastoral formation cultivates the knowledge, attitudes, and skills that directly pertain to effective functioning in the ministry setting and that also pertain to pastoral administration that supports direct ministry.*

Elements of Pastoral Formation

- *Methods for providing formation for others.* This element can be included during the human, spiritual, and intellectual formation of lay ecclesial ministers, or it can also be a separate "methods" component within their specifically pastoral formation.
- *Leading of community prayer and preaching.* Lay ecclesial ministers need to be prepared to lead community prayer in formal and informal settings, to help others participate and share in prayer leadership, and to cultivate ecumenical prayer and collaboration. They should be familiar with the Church's norms and the rites for *Holy Communion and Worship of the Eucharist Outside Mass* and for *Sunday Celebrations in the Absence of a Priest.*[92] In places and for occasions when preaching by lay persons is permissible in accord with universal law and USCCB complementary legislation, they should be encouraged to develop skills for preaching.[93]
- *Pastoral ministry skills.* This skillset includes evangelization; promotion and organization of action on behalf of justice; youth ministry; supervision or preparation of others who catechize adults, youth, or children; pastoral presence and care of the sick and dying, calling a priest for the sacraments of penance and anointing; and recognition and reporting of signs of abuse.
- *Family mission and family perspective.* The Church's vision of the role and mission of the Christian family, the meaning of married life and love, and the call to responsible parenthood should guide lay ecclesial ministers. This vision helps them attend to the social factors impinging on family life, the various contemporary forms of family configuration, and the particular importance of family in different cultural communities.

---

92 See *Holy Communion and Worship of the Eucharist Outside Mass* (New York: Catholic Book Publishing, 1976); *Sunday Celebrations in the Absence of a Priest: Bilingual Edition* (Washington, DC: USCCB, in press).

93 See CIC, canons 766-767; see also USCCB Complementary Legislation, http://www.usccb.org/norms/766.htm.

- *Effective relationship and communication skills.* Listening to others with skill, understanding and compassion is essential for the lay ecclesial minister. Equally foundational is the ability to speak to others: one on one, in small groups or in large groups, with all in the Church, and with non-Catholics and non-Christians. Lay ecclesial ministers also need to relate effectively with those whom they serve, partners (peers or those they supervise), and supervisors. Recognition and respect for different cultural styles of communication are also needed.
- *Collaboration.* We reaffirm our statement in *Called and Gifted for the Third Millennium* that "the Church's pastoral ministry can be more effective if we become true collaborators."[94] Aware of the challenges involved, we call both lay and ordained ministers to learn the skills of collaboration, to value the benefits it brings to Church life and ministry, and to commit themselves to practice it in their places of ministry.
- *Discernment of the signs of the times.* Lay ecclesial ministers should study and be familiar with current social, economic, political, and cultural situations; reflect on them in light of their doctrinal and spiritual formation; and help the faithful to do the same. Such discernment seeks to glimpse the action of the Spirit in the world and to identify resistance to the process of drawing all toward Jesus Christ, the Alpha and Omega.
- *Gift discernment and volunteer ministry management.* Lay ecclesial ministers should help the faithful discern their gifts and charisms, affirm those gifts, and nurture their call to generous service. The secular skills of volunteer management can assist ecclesial ministers in fostering the baptismal call and ministry of all the baptized. The recent decline in available volunteers in society at-large puts additional stress on Church organizations to find dedicated, qualified, and available volunteers. Because the Church will continue to need substantial numbers of volunteers to carry out its mission, paid staff (including clergy, religious, and lay persons) will need to be trained in the effective management of volunteers and to develop human resource systems, policies, and practices that often parallel those for other staff.
- *Change and conflict management skills.* Lay ecclesial ministers need to be prepared to guide others through periods of change and conflict pastorally and effectively.

---

94   *Called and Gifted for the Third Millennium*, 24.

- *Basic counseling skills.* Unless they are trained as counselors, lay ecclesial ministers should not assume that role, but they need to be able to respond to the people with active and compassionate listening, spiritual companionship, patient presence, prudent advice, and referral—and on knowing which is needed in a given situation.
- *Culture and language studies.* So that language and cultural differences will not bar anyone from receiving the pastoral ministry of the Church, we repeat what we said in *Welcoming the Stranger Among Us*: "priests, seminarians, religious, and lay ministers should all be encouraged to learn a language and acquire cultural knowledge relevant to their ministries."[95]
- *Administration skills.* Lay ecclesial ministers should develop a range of such skills as good stewardship, short- and long-range planning based on systematic analysis and theological reflection, personnel and human resource skills, budget development and management, and planning and conducting meetings. They must also be able to work with diocesan and parish systems and structures.
- *Leadership and organizational development.* Lay ecclesial ministers should cultivate leadership qualities modeled on the example of Jesus so that they can inspire and enable others to fulfill their baptismal calling.
- *Applicable civil law.* Lay ecclesial ministers need knowledge of civil law as it applies to ministerial situations.
- *Ministerial code of ethics.* Lay ecclesial ministers should know the code of ethics applicable for their ministry, abide by it, and contribute to its ongoing refinement.

Methods of Pastoral Formation

The knowledge, skills, and attitudes necessary for pastoral ministry may be taught in traditional classroom or seminar formats, but that is not enough. The teaching must be supplemented by practical experience in real situations and by mentored reflection on those experiences. These experiences include opportunities to practice skills with feedback, as well as demonstrations, projects and practica, and role playing.

---

95   USCCB, *Welcoming the Stranger Among Us: Unity in Diversity* (Washington, DC: USCCB, 2000), 37.

Integrating the Four Elements of Formation

Although the four elements of formation (human, spiritual, intellectual, and pastoral) have been addressed separately, they must be integrated as a unified whole in the person of the well-formed lay ecclesial minister, which happens best if these elements are integrated in the formation program itself.

Such integration can be fostered through *guided pastoral practice*—field experience or a practicum requiring the learner to put into practice what has been learned, drawing consciously on all four dimensions of formation in planning, implementing, and evaluating a project of ministerial service. The role of the mentor or supervisor is essential here, guiding the learner to reflect upon, understand, and grow from the lived experience of ministry.

A *shared formation program vision*—cultivating a common sense of purpose, goals, identity, and program spirit among all the formators, whatever dimensions of formation they are responsible for—can also contribute to the successful integration of the four dimensions in the experience of the learner. Whether through team meetings, written program materials, consultation with the program director, or social interactions and the building of relationships among formators, it is important that all who provide formation realize the vision, principles, and components of the total formation process and how they are to be integrated. In this way, each formator can coordinate his or her component with the whole.

Finally, the actual *practice of ministry* is a powerful occasion for ongoing formation and provides a valuable opportunity for integration. Theological reflection upon such ministry practice makes possible "a general and integral process of constant growth, deepening each of the aspects of formation—human, spiritual, intellectual and pastoral—as well as ensuring their active and harmonious integration, based on pastoral charity and in reference to it."[96]

Ongoing Formation

Initial formation ideally precedes one's exercise of the responsibilities of ecclesial ministry and prepares one for it. Ongoing formation continues the process of learning and growing throughout the time one serves in ministry. For many lay ecclesial ministers who come to formation programs with much ministry experi-

---

96   PDV, no. 71.

ence, the lines between these two are blurred, but that does not diminish the importance of continuing to develop all areas of formation.

Ongoing formation, which strengthens ministerial identity as well as enhancing ministerial skills, is not a luxury to be pursued when time and resources allow, but is rather a permanent necessity for every ecclesial minister, lay or ordained. No lay ecclesial minister should feel excused from taking part in it; failure to do so represents neglect of a significant ministerial responsibility. As a matter of course, bishops require ongoing formation of all lay ecclesial ministers; their pastors or supervisors expect and encourage it; and their local communities support it. It is helpful when diocesan and parish personnel policies and practices make regular provision both for time away and for some allotment of funding assistance for formation whenever possible.

While on some occasions laity, religious, deacons, and priests need to address issues unique to their own states of life and the implications of those issues for their ministry, experiences of ongoing formation that include all ministers can help build the relationships that are key to collaboration in ministry.

Ongoing formation can occur in many forms:

- Diocesan, regional, or national conferences, and active participation in the work of diocesan, regional, and national ministerial associations
- Immersion experiences (e.g., in other cultures)
- Further academic coursework and ministry-specific skill development training, either in person or online; ongoing personal reading and reading of ministry periodicals and journals
- Continuing theological reflection on the practice of ministry
- Diocesan or parish staff workshops, renewal days, short courses, study weeks, or retreats
- Support groups, study groups, or book clubs
- A relationship with a mentor and/or spiritual director

In addition, teaching, giving workshops, and mentoring others are also means of continuing growth for oneself, as well as a contribution to the ministerial life of the wider Church. Sabbaticals for lay ecclesial ministers who have given long and significant service to a particular diocesan church recognize their service and provide an opportunity for extended ongoing formation, invigorating and expanding their ability to serve in the future.

The ongoing formational needs of lay ecclesial ministers may change over the course of a long career. Those beginning in ministry may need extra advice and encouragement to face the new situations that test their abilities and calling. Those more experienced may need spiritual renewal if ministry has become routine or tinged with a certain weariness, tedium or even cynicism. Those entering a new area of ministry may need some review in all four dimensions of formation in the context of the new ministry. Those nearing retirement may find rejuvenation through being asked and helped to become mentors for those newer in ministry.

Agents of Formation

The Holy Spirit is the principal agent of formation: the Spirit of Jesus, sent by the Father, given in Baptism, poured out anew in Confirmation, bestowing personal gifts and charisms on each of the faithful, to be developed and used in the service of others (see 1 Cor 12:7, 1 Pt 4:10). When lay ecclesial ministers cultivate a special devotion and complete openness to the Holy Spirit, the power of Pentecost will be alive in their hearts and at work through their ministry.

The bishop is the chief shepherd and teacher of his diocese, responsible for ensuring that lay ecclesial ministers are well prepared and competent to carry out their ministerial roles and functions. Carefully choosing programs that are in accord with Church teaching and approving programs of preparation, the bishop sets high standards for the sake of excellence in ministry, expecting and assisting lay ecclesial ministers to meet such standards. Regular communication between diocesan representatives and those institutions preparing lay ecclesial ministers is particularly desirable. The bishop also recognizes special situations in his diocese where exceptions may be called for. He ensures that diocesan personnel policies and budget decisions support lay ecclesial ministers' efforts to meet these standards; he expects and assists parish policies and practices to do the same. He gives witness to these values by the personal example of his own ongoing formation for his ministry, his spirituality, and his dedication to a holy life. In all these ways he works persistently to build up the life of the diocese by strengthening the quality of its ministries and the competence of its ministers.

Pastors and other supervisors should look upon lay ecclesial ministers as valued co-workers in ministry. They should allow, encourage, and support their initial and ongoing formation for ministry. Pastors should be able to look to their bishop and his staff (in ministry formation, human resources, stewardship, development, or other diocesan offices) for advice and assistance in dealing with such efforts.

The local community where lay ecclesial ministers serve should be helped to recognize the value of their ministry and be encouraged to provide personal and financial support. Parishioners can provide personal support through recognition and affirmation for the ministry that lay ecclesial ministers provide; and they can provide financial support through contributions to the parish that make possible just compensation for pastoral staff, financial assistance toward their formation, and subsequent compensation commensurate with increased competency acquired through formation.

Diocesan formation program administrators are responsible for curriculum design, formator recruitment, financial assistance, and other tasks that make possible a high quality and accessible formation program. In colleges, seminaries, and universities, those responsibilities are often widely distributed. It is particularly helpful for small and rural dioceses to collaborate with one another and with other institutions to develop the resources that will provide excellent formation.

Formators themselves are responsible for designing and implementing learning experiences through which program participants acquire the knowledge, competence, and spirit for ministry. Formators need to have appropriate academic credentials, at the doctoral or at least the master's level, and need to demonstrate proven competence in their discipline of study. Catholics who teach theological subjects must, like other Catholics, "live lives of faith within the community and in fidelity to the teaching authority of the Church."[97] "Catholics who teach theological disciplines in a Catholic university are required to have a *mandatum* granted by the competent ecclesiastical authority."[98] Personal experience in Church ministry is helpful. Excellence in teaching is to be desired.

All formation is ultimately self-formation,[99] and lay ecclesial ministers themselves are the pivotal agents of their own formation. We call them to nurture in themselves a deep and powerful hunger for formation, willingness to learn and grow, and desire to serve the Lord with excellence and generosity.

---

97   USCCB, *Doctrinal Responsibilities* (Washington, DC: USCCB, 1989), 5, citing LG, no. 25.

98   USCCB, *The Application of Ex Corde Ecclesiae for the United States*, Part II, Art. 4, no. 4e (Washington, DC: USCCB, 2000); see also *Guidelines Concerning the Academic Mandatum in Catholic Universities* (Washington, DC: USCCB, 2001).

99   See CL, no. 63; PDV, no. 69.

C. Authorization for Lay Ecclesial Ministry

While all members of the lay Christian faithful work to further the Church's mission, some are entrusted with certain offices and roles connected to the ministry of the ordained pastors. The lay women and men who are given these responsibilities are not only distinguished by particular gifts and a willingness to serve the Church—these qualities could apply to all the laity—but are also responding to a call to work in greater collaboration with ordained ministers. They are authorized by ecclesiastical authorities to carry out certain ministerial responsibilities in public service of the local church.

This chapter focuses on those lay ecclesial ministers who exercise their ministry within parish communities. However, the principles and strategies suggested here may also be considered for their relevance to other settings in which lay ecclesial ministers serve.

Authorization is the process by which properly prepared lay men and women are given responsibilities for ecclesial ministry by competent Church authority. This process includes the following elements: acknowledgment of the competence of an individual for a specific ministerial role (often called "certification"); appointment of an individual to a specific position (in some dioceses called "commissioning"), along with a delineation of the obligations, responsibilities, and authority of that position (and length of term, if specified); and finally an announcement of the appointment to the community that will be served by the lay ecclesial minister.

Because it involves a formal, public confirmation of the call to ecclesial ministry, the authorization process might be considered the final result of the personal and ecclesial discernment discussed earlier in this document.

Given the varying circumstances of each diocese—its pastoral needs and financial and educational resources—it is important that the diocesan bishop be responsible for determining if and how any authorization should occur in his diocese, in keeping with canon law. When such authorization does occur, it is important to emphasize a spiritual dimension within the process.

The Role of the Bishop in the Authorization of Lay Ecclesial Ministers

Entrusted with the pastoral care of all within his diocese, the diocesan bishop oversees all catechetical (CIC, canon 386), liturgical (canon 387), and apostolic works (canon 394) carried out in the diocese, and he enjoys the authority necessary to meet these responsibilities (canon 381).[100] In this capacity he ensures the suitability of candidates to take on roles that are critical to the proper care of souls. He may do so directly (for example, the office of pastor [canon 524]) or through others (for example, teachers of religion [canon 805]).

Just as the diocesan bishop oversees the preparation of priests and deacons of the diocese, he is rightly attentive to the proper preparation of the growing number of lay women and men who minister in the Church. This oversight includes attention to the selection of those who will serve and their adequate preparation. His authorization demonstrates to the community in which they serve that their work has his confidence and support.

The Role of the Pastor in the Authorization Process

The diocesan bishop entrusts to the pastor of a parish the responsibility of providing pastoral care to all within the parish, under the authority of the diocesan bishop and with the cooperation of other priests and deacons and the assistance of the laity (CIC, canon 519). Even parochial vicars, who are assigned by the bishop to assist in the pastoral care of a parish, and whose rights and obligations are established by universal and particular law, work within the structure of ministry established by the pastor (canons 545, 548). The pastor thus has great latitude in organizing parish resources to meet the pastoral needs of the people.

The support of the pastor has been found crucial to the success of lay ecclesial ministry within parish communities.[101] This suggests that although the diocesan bishop may oversee the authorization process, the unique role of the pastor in selecting those who will serve on the pastoral team should be acknowledged.

---

100 See Second Vatican Council, *Decree on the Pastoral Office of the Bishops in the Church* (*Christus Dominus*), no. 8.

101 See Philip Murnion, *New Parish Ministers: Laity and Religious on Parish Staffs* (New York: National Pastoral Life Center, 1992), 55-65.

Specific Roles Covered by the Authorization Process

A diocese must first identify those roles that, in the judgment of the diocesan bishop, are so essential to collaborating in the pastoral care of people that diocesan policies are needed to ensure that those who are given these roles have the appropriate education, formation, experience, and ecclesial recognition to meet the needs of the community. This is true regardless of whether the lay ecclesial minister is a paid staff member or a volunteer. The nature of ministerial responsibilities is what determines the importance of authorization, not whether the lay ecclesial minister is salaried.

The Certification of Candidates for Lay Ecclesial Ministry Positions

Ensuring the quality of pastoral care provided by lay ecclesial ministers requires a process for deciding that a given candidate has the education, formation, and professional skills necessary to serve in a particular role. This involves establishing the requirements for education, formation, and experience for specific ministerial roles and evaluating the extent to which individuals meet these requirements. This may vary from diocese to diocese, but the competence of those who serve needs to be verified in some way.

The diocesan bishop has several options for setting certification requirements. Some examples for specific ministry roles can be found in the certification standards established by national associations serving lay ministers in general or role-specific sub-groups and approved by the USCCB Commission on Certification and Accreditation.[102] Among the criteria the diocese might use in deciding how flexible these requirements can be are the availability of existing formation programs within the diocese or region, the financial and personnel resources of the diocese, the size and location of the diocese, and changing pastoral needs. In all cases, the requirements should be clearly stated and readily accessible to those interested in preparing for lay ecclesial ministry and to those who lead existing programs.

The diocese can establish a program that candidates must complete prior to consideration for service within the diocese. Some formation programs have fruitfully sought and received accreditation by the USCCB Commission on

---

102 See p. 30 note 64.

Certification and Accreditation.[103] Alternatively, a list of acceptable programs can be developed that meet diocesan requirements and that provide multiple options for scheduling and class location.

The certification of an individual for a specific position may be accomplished at one of two points in the authorization process. The qualifications of a given candidate can be examined at the time he or she is being considered for a given position. Alternatively, some dioceses establish a list of persons who have submitted their credentials and are judged qualified for various positions; parishes may give priority or restrict consideration to those persons.

Whenever possible, provinces or regions can develop consistent certification standards and procedures so that lay ecclesial ministers might transfer from one diocese to another in the region with the approval of the sending and receiving bishops.

The Appointment of Lay Ecclesial Ministers

The appointment of a person to a specific position should be done in writing (required for ecclesiastical offices [CIC, canon 156]) and should include the rights and obligations attached to the position or office, any limits on the exercise of authority (e.g., budget reviews, prior permission for certain actions), relevant employment and personnel policies, any limitations on the term of the appointment, and—perhaps most importantly—any special delegation to perform functions proper to the ordained (e.g., baptizing outside of emergencies [canon 861 §2] and witnessing the exchange of matrimonial consent [canon 1112§1][104]). Legal counsel should be consulted with respect to the drafting of written contracts and/or any proposed term of appointment.

Use of terminology drawn from canon law can promote consistency within and among diocesan practices. For example, the word "entrust" is generally used for those who hold an office in which there is great discretion concerning specific programs and methods—for example, a diocese is entrusted to a bishop (CIC, canon 369), or pastoral care in a parish may be entrusted to a single pastor (canon 515), to several priests *in solidum* (canon 517 §1), or to a religious institute (canon 520); or participation in this care can be entrusted to deacons or laypersons (canon 517 §2).

---

103 Programs at other institutions (seminaries, theological schools, universities) are accredited by other agencies, e.g., the Association of Theological Schools or regional accrediting associations.

104 See USCCB Complementary Legislation, http://www.usccb.org/norms/1112.htm.

Several terms refer to the filling of an ecclesiastical office, defined in law as a function constituted in a stable manner for a spiritual purpose (see CIC, canon 145). The law refers to an office's being *conferred* by a proper authority (canon 147), to the making of canonical *provision* for an office (canons 146, 147), and to someone's *appointment* to a specific office (e.g., chancellors [canon 482], tribunal judges [canon 1421], and so on). The rights and obligations inherent to a specific office come with the provision of the office itself and cease with the loss of the office.

Since not every ministry within the Church has been constituted as an ecclesiastical office, caution is advisable before establishing lay ecclesial ministries in this manner. Those who hold ecclesiastical offices enjoy a certain stability in office. Bishops might instead consider prescribing terms of service for the exercise of certain responsibilities within the Church. Specifying a term of service (which of course can be renewed) also provides flexibility for a newly installed bishop or newly appointed pastor to make key personnel assignments after a period of transition.

The term "mandate" is generally used when someone is appointed for a specific instance: for example, to act as an advocate for a party in a judicial matter (canon 1484) or when someone has received some responsibility that properly belongs to an office he or she does not hold (canon 142 addresses the cessation of delegated power when a specific mandate has been fulfilled). "Delegation" generally refers to a situation where someone who has ordinary executive power by virtue of an office permits someone else to exercise that power in general or in specific situations.

The bishop may reserve to himself the rights to review the credentials of a candidate or meet the candidate before an appointment is made. He may, however, grant to the one who has overall responsibility for pastoral care—for example, a pastor in parish ministry—the necessary authority to appoint someone as a lay ecclesial minister.

The means used to announce an appointment to lay ecclesial ministry can follow the procedures used in announcing other similar personnel changes within the diocese. In most circumstances, publication of the appointment in the diocesan newspaper, clergy newsletter, or parish bulletin or newsletter may be all that is needed, so long as such an announcement provides a clear statement of the role, responsibilities, and authority of the newly appointed lay ecclesial minister.

Blessings and Rituals in the Authorization Process

At certain points in the authorization process, public prayer and ritual can be significant for the lay ecclesial minister and for the community, highlighting the new relationships that the person is beginning in the life of the community. Models for this already exist in the commissioning ceremony for catechists called for in the *National Directory for Catechesis*.[105] The recognition of those who have met certification requirements for lay ecclesial ministry is often done within the context of a special Liturgy.

A public ceremony or Liturgy for the conferral of an office emphasizes the relationship of the diocesan bishop with the lay ecclesial minister and the community to be served. In particular, a public ritual would be of great significance when deacons, religious, or lay persons are entrusted with a participation in the pastoral care of a parish (under canon 517 §2). Whatever rite is used for the latter situation, it should be clear that the person appointed is not a substitute for the priest who directs the pastoral care of the parish, nor should the impression be given that it is the rite itself that confers the appointment.

For lay ecclesial ministers who serve in parishes in roles other than that provided for in CIC, canon 517 §2 (see above), the use of ritual in presenting the lay ecclesial minister to the community can underscore the importance of this person's role in the life of the community and provide opportunity for the lay ecclesial minister and the community to pray together. Since the Church deeply values ritual blessings and communal prayer, such a celebration would both instruct the community and spiritually strengthen the lay ecclesial minister. Part VI of the *Book of Blessings* provides several orders for blessings that can be used or adapted to meet the particular needs of the parish or diocese.

Additional Considerations

Establishing a formal process for authorizing lay women and men for key positions of ecclesial ministry can give the diocesan bishop greater confidence that the spiritual needs of the portion of the People of God entrusted to his care will be met. That process will differ between dioceses depending on the availability of formation programs and the need to provide ministerial opportunities for immigrant or

---

105 See USCCB, *National Directory for Catechesis* (Washington, DC: USCCB, 2005), Section 55, "Preparation and Ongoing Formation of Catechists."

transient communities or those located in less affluent areas of the diocese. Any process for certifying the qualifications of candidates should include a provision for accepting experience in lieu of coursework for those whose service predates education and formation requirements. Provision should also be made for evaluating and recognizing academic credentials and ministerial experience acquired outside the United States. Furthermore, flexibility is needed so that volunteers who have experience within the parish and the personal and professional qualities needed in ministry are not excluded from consideration for these ministerial positions, especially in parishes without resources to hire professional staff.

Most importantly, the authorization process can provide occasions for the bishop to demonstrate his support for the lay ecclesial ministers of his diocese and to model collaboration with them as his lay co-workers.

D. The Ministerial Workplace

Context

The diversity among our dioceses is particularly relevant to workplace issues. We acknowledge that many dioceses have well-developed human resource departments, while others are in the initial stages of developing policies. We also acknowledge that not all employees of the diocese or a parish wish to be, or are in fact considered, lay ecclesial ministers. The following ideas are to be evaluated by individual dioceses in light of their own circumstances. These comments are not intended to be prescriptive or normative.

We are grateful that lay persons have responded to the call to ecclesial ministry in such great numbers. Without them the work of the Church would be seriously diminished. Lay ecclesial ministers—and indeed all lay Church employees and volunteers—function in a workplace that shares both the characteristics of a faith community of co-workers, as described by St. Paul, and the characteristics of a modern organization. Thus, in the ministerial workplace, one finds the special challenge of establishing policies and practices that integrate Gospel values and best organizational practices. This is particularly true as regards the management of human resources.

Best organizational practices are consistent with Gospel values. They balance the goals and needs of the organization, its workers and the community in which it is located. They imply respect for persons, justice, integrity, efficient use of resources, successful accomplishment of mission and goals, and an environment in which committed and skilled workers are treated fairly. Furthermore, the *Code of Canon Law*, particularly in its treatment of temporal and human resources, provides prescriptions that are to be followed for best organizational practice in an ecclesial context (see CIC, canons 1273ff.).

The growing presence of lay ecclesial ministers and other lay workers in Church institutions has prompted some dioceses to develop comprehensive personnel systems, with beneficial results. Such a system "includes both the variety of people serving in the Church (lay people, sisters, brothers, deacons, priests) and the range of personnel functions."[106] Further, "comprehensiveness does not seek to apply the

---

106 *Just Treatment for Those Who Work for the Church* (Cincinnati, OH: National Association of Church Personnel Administrators [NACPA], 1986), 1.

same policy to all groups, but rather to create consistent policies, coming from the same basic philosophical stance, which takes into consideration the needs of all . . . groups, and indeed the interests of the entire Church."[107]

Some Human Resource Areas in a Comprehensive Personnel System

Six human resource areas are typically dealt with in a comprehensive human resource system. These areas, highlighted here, have particular significance for lay ecclesial ministers who make their living in the Church.

As with the suggestions in preceding sections of this document, the following ideas will need to be evaluated by each diocese in light of its own circumstances.

1. *Recruitment and selection.* This area frequently addresses the value of posting job openings, having written position descriptions, and, when appropriate, using search committees of people who are trained in interview skills, know which questions are permissible and not permissible in an interview, make careful use of references, and are familiar with anti-discrimination laws. In the "Pathways," "Formation," and "Authorization" sections of this document are found other considerations relevant to this function.

2. *Orientation and support for new lay ecclesial ministers.* People new to any organization need to understand its mission, culture, and history and need to meet other workers in order to bring their gifts to bear on the organization. The nature of the orientation will vary depending on the individual's previous experience, the level of responsibility to be assumed, and the workplace in which they serve. This orientation can include an introduction to the particular parish and to the diocese.

   Supports would include reasonable accommodations made in the workplace for lay ecclesial ministers with disabilities who are otherwise qualified to carry out their ministry.

---

107 *The Individual and the Institution: Strengthening Working Relationships in the Church* (Cincinnati, OH: NACPA, 1994), 10.

3. *Evaluation and feedback.* In a comprehensive personnel system, this area addresses regular performance appraisals, as a part of ministerial workplace practice, that provide a formal opportunity for every individual minister to reflect on his or her own performance and get feedback from a supervisor and that may include the views of colleagues and those served. Appraisal and feedback is most effective when conducted in the context of the mission of the parish or diocese. Documentation of honest and constructive feedback about deficiencies and subsequent steps for improvement is important, as is both formal and informal recognition of generous, Christ-centered, and effective service.

4. *Compensation.* While not all those working for the Church are paid, all deserve recognition and affirmation of their contribution to its mission. Those lay ecclesial ministers serving in paid positions need fair compensation for their work.[108] The Church has a long history of speaking about the dignity of work and the proper recognition of people's service. In a comprehensive personnel system, this area includes salary plans that may establish ranges through which individuals may progress, as well as benefit plans (e.g., health insurance, family leave, child care assistance, funding for ongoing education). These issues can be particularly challenging when resources are limited. Compensation packages vary from one geographic region to another depending on the finances of each diocese and the cost of living in a given area.

A comprehensive personnel system may also include agreed-upon expectations about the time given to ministry—a particularly sensitive issue for lay ecclesial ministers since so much Church ministry takes place on weekends or evenings. Another area that is important to lay workers is portability of benefits because of the mobility of some lay ecclesial ministers. Some groups of dioceses have begun to develop programs that respond to this reality.

---

108   See CIC, canons 231 §2, 1286 2°. Two thirds of parish ministers either strongly agreed (22.5 percent) or agreed somewhat (45.7 percent) that their annual earnings were adequate for their personal, family, or religious congregational needs; 31.8 percent reported that they did not find them adequate; and 37.8 percent indicated that they do not believe that their parishes have the resources to compensate them adequately (DeLambo [2005], 127-128).

5. *Transitions and terminations.* When a lay ecclesial minister enters the service of the Church, it is often hoped that they will continue in such service over time.[109] As pastors change, these lay ecclesial ministers can both offer support to the departing pastor and help to orient the new pastor and assist him and the people of the parish in building new relationships. It may be desirable in some situations that the term of a lay ecclesial minister conclude, even if subject to renewal, when the pastor's term of office comes to an end. The potential for tension is present in every transition. The diocese can be helpful in the process of clarifying expectations and assisting in conflict resolution. When a lay ecclesial minister is the one making a transition or ending service, such practices as exit interviews can help the parish or diocese learn from the lay ecclesial minister's experience. Outplacement and severance assistance can make the time of transition less stressful for the individual.

6. *Grievance procedures.* This area usually includes resources for dispute resolution that—when used early enough and made available in the Church workplace—can often reduce or resolve tensions that might lead to voluntary departure or dismissal.[110] Grievance procedures provide an objective process for addressing good faith claims by those who think they have been unfairly treated.

Resources and Outcomes

The diocese, under the leadership of its bishop, is the primary support for pastoral ministry in the diocese. The diocese can also be a model for the parishes in human resource administration. Since most parishes do not have adequate resources to manage human resources professionally, they look to the diocese for guidance. In some instances dioceses also lack sufficient resources, yet they can benefit from some effort to assist parishes in these areas.

Other dioceses have significant resources that support a comprehensive human resource system throughout the diocese, ensuring, for instance, that comparable parish positions filled by lay ecclesial ministers have comparable salaries and benefits. Diocesan staff may serve as a resource in recruiting parish staff and providing orientation for new employees. They may offer periodic training sessions.

---

109 Of full-time lay persons in parish ministry, 79.4 percent report that they believe they are pursuing a lifetime in Church ministry, up 9.5 percent from 1997; and 62 percent of part-time lay persons report having the same belief, up 11 percent from 1997 (DeLambo [2005], 71).

110 See USCCB, *Procedures for Resolving Conflict* (Washington, DC: USCCB, 2002).

Larger dioceses and those that provide significant support in the area of human resources to the parishes—working closely with pastors, those entrusted with the pastoral care of a parish, and parish business managers—may need several human resource professional and support staff members.

When centralized diocesan support is not in place, clusters of parishes or diocesan associations of parish administrators with responsibility for human resources can be a significant resource for parish staffs. State Catholic conferences and state or regional associations of diocesan human resource directors can be helpful for training, sharing ideas and experience, and addressing state legislation that impacts the church workplace. On the national level, the National Association of Church Personnel Administrators is a significant resource, assisting in the integration of Gospel values with best organizational practices in human resource management.

Such integration can bring about many outcomes: improved morale among lay ecclesial ministers, savings of time and money and avoidance of fracturing the community in the resolution of employee disputes, and the successful recruitment and retention of qualified and committed lay ecclesial ministers. Most importantly, they will provide a model where the People of God are nourished in their faith and where the Catholic diocese and its parishes witness, for the local community, to a workplace that integrates Gospel values and best organizational practices.

Conclusion

The same God who called Prisca and Aquila to work with Paul in the first century calls thousands of men and women to minister in our Church in this twenty-first century. This call is a cause for rejoicing. It is also an occasion for the kind of planning that Pope John Paul II recommended in *Novo Millennio Ineunte*:

> The program already exists: it is the plan found in the Gospel and in the living tradition, it is the same as ever. Ultimately, it has its center in Christ himself, who is to be known, loved and imitated, so that in him we may live the life of the Trinity, and with him transform history until its fulfillment in the heavenly Jerusalem. This is a program which does not change with shifts of times and cultures, even though it takes account of time and culture for the sake of true dialogue and effective communication. This program for all times is our program for the Third Millennium.

> But it must be translated into *pastoral initiatives adapted to the circumstances of each community.* . . . It is *in the local churches* that the specific features of a detailed pastoral plan can be identified—goals and methods, formation and enrichment of the people involved, the search for the necessary resources—which will enable the proclamation of Christ to reach people, mold communities, and have a deep and incisive influence in bringing Gospel values to bear in society and culture.[111]

Co-Workers in the Vineyard of the Lord is intended as one resource for that kind of planning. We recognize that our document does not address every issue related to lay ecclesial ministry or anticipate every possibility for recognizing, developing, and integrating the gifts that lay leaders bring to our Church. There is need for each diocese to review its own situation and for each diocese or region to develop appropriate plans.

---

111 NMI, no. 29.

Within the next five years it will be helpful to revisit the material here and refine it in the light of our experience. The preparation of *Co-Workers in the Vineyard of the Lord* has already indicated a need for a more thorough study of our theology of vocation, and some have asked for a common title for those people appointed under CIC, canon 517 §2—both of which are beyond the scope of this document.

In the interim we will approach the challenge of responding to lay ecclesial ministry with the same fresh energy and creativity that the Holy Father called for later in his apostolic letter:

> Let us go forward in hope! A new millennium is opening before the Church like a vast ocean upon which we shall venture, relying on the help of Christ. The Son of God, who became incarnate two thousand years ago out of love for humanity, is at work even today: we need discerning eyes to see this and, above all, a generous heart to become the instruments of his work.[112]

We are blessed indeed to have such gifted and generous co-workers in the vineyard of the Lord to which we have all been called. Let us continue to work together as a "community of people united in Christ and guided by the holy Spirit in [our] pilgrimage toward the Father's kingdom, bearers of a message for all humanity."[113]

---

112 NMI, no. 58.

113 GS, no. 1.